My Dearest Friend

Thanks for your support!

Mike Lewing

My Dearest Friend

The Civil War Correspondence of
Cornelia McGimsey and
Lewis Warlick

Edited by
Mike and Carolyn Lawing

CAROLINA ACADEMIC PRESS
Durham, North Carolina

ISBN 0-89089-832-4
LCCN 99-069190

CAROLINA ACADEMIC PRESS
700 Kent Street
Durham, North Carolina 27701
Telephone (919) 489-7486
Fax (919) 493-5668
www.cap-press.com

Printed in the United States of America

Contents

Acknowledgments

A special thanks to:

- Mr. and Mrs. Jimmy Furr (Mary Lou Avery Furr) for providing the hospitality of their home and a visit to Canoe Hill. Mrs. Furr generously shared two photographs of Laura Cornelia McGimsey, photocopies of three letters, which were not part of the McGimsey Papers, and a copy of the proclamation of Governor Ellis.

- Mr. Roy Avery who owns and maintains the old house and cemetery at Canoe Hill. "Cousin Roy" provided the tractor and his personal guided tour down the muddy road to Canoe Hill.

- The Burke County Genealogical Society and Mrs. Mary Jane Simmons in particular for publishing some of these letters in the *Journal*.

- Dr. Richard Shrader at the Southern Historical Collection, Wilson Library, The University of North Carolina at Chapel Hill.

- Mr. Ralph Morrison for providing copies of two letters written by his ancestor from Point Lookout Prison.

- Ms. Linda Garibaldi, Curator, N.C. Room, Burke County Public Library.

- Mrs. Martha McGimsey Lawing, my mother, who provided many wonderful visits to her brothers, sisters, aunts, uncles, and cousins and allowed me to listen to their stories of "Old Burke."

Introduction

Laura Cornelia McGimsey was the older of two daughters born to Joseph Lewis McGimsey and his second wife, Elizabeth Alexander McGimsey. By the time she came along on November 1, 1840, her father was a 65-year-old farmer who had already raised five children and five stepchildren with his first wife, Allie Moore Wakefield McGimsey. Both of Cornelia's parents died in the 1850s, her father in 1852 and her mother in 1859. When these letters were written, she and her younger sister Celeste were living at Pleasant Hill, the home place. They shared the home with an older half brother, Alpheus McGimsey and his family, and a much older stepbrother, John Wakefield, whom she always referred to as "Uncle John."

Cornelia's best beau was John Lewis Warlick, son of John and Elizabeth Baker Warlick of Table Rock, N.C. Although their courtship had some rough spots, and Cornelia did correspond with at least one other beau, Lewis prevailed and their courtship became a marriage. Their courtship had begun at least a year before the war. Lewis wrote one letter to her in 1860 while he was on a trip through western North Carolina and north Georgia.

Abraham Lincoln's election to the presidency in 1860 ignited secession in South Carolina. Both pro union and pro-secession meetings were held in Burke County and thirty other counties across North Carolina. Pro-unionists correctly argued that a Democratically controlled House and Senate would keep the President from enacting any anti–southern legislation. By the end of January that majority vanished when six additional southern states seceded. North Carolina was not anxious for secession or war. In February 1861 the voters defeated a proposal to call a convention to consider secession. The western part of the state was more pro-union than any other section. When war did come, North Carolina was the tenth of eleven southern states to secede.

The first Civil War military company organized from Burke County was the "Burke Rifles." J. Lewis Warlick mustered in as a corporal. The company was enrolled for active service at Morganton, N.C. on April 18, 1861.

It arrived in Raleigh, N.C. April 25th and was mustered into State service on May 13th as Company G, in the First Regiment North Carolina Volunteers, "for the term of six months..." The 11th Regiment N.C. Troops became the successor of the First Regiment. Many of the men from Company G re-enlisted in Companies B and D of the new regiment.

This correspondence in the Southern Historical Collection is generally between Lewis Warlick while in the Confederate Infantry and Laura Cornelia McGimsey back home at Pleasant Hill, on the Linville River. The conversation between a man and a woman is all there, as though it has been waiting for someone to listen. Letters from others occasionally offer other perspectives.

The men and women of North Carolina who penned these letters and passed these stories from generation to generation wrote this book. These letters open a window to the lives of several families living in Burke County, North Carolina during the Civil War. The original grammar and spelling of the letters have been retained.

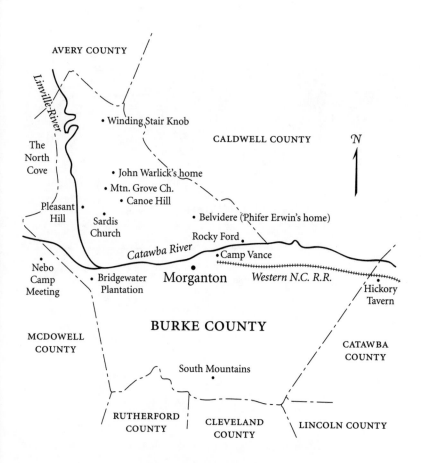

Map of Burke County, North Carolina

Places mentioned in the letters. Only railroads that are mentioned are shown here.

STATE OF NORTH CAROLINA.
A PROCLAMATION,
BY JOHN W. ELLIS,
GOVERNOR OF NORTH CAROLINA

WHEREAS: By Proclamation of Abraham Lincoln, President of the United States, followed by a requisition of Simon Cameron, Secretary of War, I am informed that the said Abraham Lincoln has made a call for 75,000 men to be employed for the invasion of the peaceful homes of the South, and for the violent subversion of the liberties of a free people, constituting a large part of the whole population of the late United States: And, whereas, this high-handed act of tyrannical outrage is not only in violation of all constitutional law, in utter disregard of every sentiment of humanity and Christian civilization, and conceived in a spirit of aggression unparalleled by any act of recorded history, but is a direct step towards the subjugation of the whole South, and the conversion of a free Republic, inherited from our fathers, into a military despotism, to be established by worse than foreign enemies on the ruins of our once glorious Constitution of Equal Rights.

Now, therefore, I, JOHN W. ELLIS, Governor of the State of North-Carolina, for these extraordinary causes, do hereby issue this, my Proclamation, notifying and requesting the Senators and Members of the House of Commons of the General Assembly of North-Carolina, to meet in Special Session at the Capitol, in the City of Raleigh, on Wednesdey the first day of May next. And I furthermore exhort all good citizens throughout the State to be mindful that their first allegiance is due to the Sovereignty which protects their homes and dearest interests, as their first service is due for the sacred defence of their hearths, and of the soil which holds the graves of our glorious dead.

United action in defence of the sovereignty of North-Carolina, and of the rights of the South, becomes now the duty of all.

Given under my hand, and attested by the Great Seal of the State. Done at the City of Raleigh, the 17th day of April; A. D., 1861, and in the eighty-fifth year of our Independence,

JOHN. W. ELLIS.

By the Governor,

GRAHAM DAVES, *Private Secretary.*

My Dearest Friend

Chapter 1

The First Six Months of War
and the
Folks Back Home

Linville River N.C.
May the 6th / 61

My dearest friend,

I received your kind letter last mail, I hasten a reply thinking you would like to hear from me; I was glad to hear that you were enjoying yourself and were all well, you said you were anxious to leave Dry Ponds, perhaps it was best to go to Raleigh but I did not like to hear of you going further off. I fear the next news I hear you will be going to Washington city   you say it is ours and we ought to have it. I admit that, but what would it profit you or me if you were to loose your life in the struggle.

I saw two more volunteering yesterday   John and Hutsell Wise they belong to Z. B. Vance's company   he will pass down the Asheville road today   they say they have 96 of the best men in N.C. their average weight is 168 pounds and are about his (Vance's) highth, my little friend Jim Gudger is along and several more of my acquaintance, cousin Theodore Erwin is married   he married Callie Wells. I am going to tell him that he married to keep from going to war. Miss Polly McCall of the North Cove stopped her lover from going to war Mr. James English had volunteered and started   he called to say goodbye to Miss McCall   she was washing when he came, she told him that he should not go, but that they would get married   it is said that he threw down his knapsack and helped her to wring out the clothes   they were married the same evening; I think that is what you might call taking a wife out of the suds. I expect a good many of us would of said as she did had we followed our own inclinations, but circumstances told us that would not do. We are expecting Capt. McElroy's company down this road Wednesday   I am anxious to see them pass, his company numbers one hundred. Sid Conley volunteered but has been sick ever since   you doubtedly will say that he got sick to keep from going   I think he intended going, and could not help getting sick. Dr. Hapboldt has been visiting him. — Well Lewis it does seem to me like I had parted with every friend I had on earth you said you were all lively and in good spirits   I was glad to hear it indeed, but I do tell you it is more than I can say of those you left behind, it has been two weeks to day since I saw you   it seems to me

like two months was shorter before you left than two weeks now   I
do not know how the summer will pass if you do not get back soon
and there is not much prospect of you getting back soon if ever — I
have not seen any of the Irish creek folks since you left   I suppose
they will be up at Sardis next Sunday if nothing happens where we
will see each other   for my part I am not going because I want to go,
but because I think it my duty to go   how strange it will look to see
all your seats vacant   three weeks before we were all together, now we
are separated, and in three weeks more there is no telling where we
will be.

Will we ever meet again. If negatived   Oh!   Hate relent and bid
us meet once more.

Monday evening   I have heard this evening Mr. Bob Patton is to
be married next Sunday   I do not know whether it is so or not. It has
been raining all day today and yesterday too   I would be glad to have
clear weather again for dull weather makes me feel more lonely than I
would if it was clear — I do not want you and cousin Bob to forget
your promise to me to be good boys, and let me beg of you, for my
sake not to rush into danger when it is avoidable.

I will quit writing for I know I have written more than you wish
to read, ... It was better I am ashamed of this letter, but if you will
excuse me this time I will try to do better in the future   I would write
every week if I knew where to direct to, please write soon, sooner,
soonest to your

ever affectionate friend
Cornelia

P. S. give my respects to cousin Bob, Tom Parks, and Port Warlick   I
would be pleased to hear from them.

Dry Ponds was a small community in Lincoln County that Lewis visited before leaving for Raleigh.

Sardis Church was an interdenominational church, which served black and white Baptists, Methodists and Presbyterians. After the War Between the States these groups formed their own churches and Sardis was torn down.

Cousin Bob was Robert Vance Kerley, later a 2nd Lieutenant in Company B, 54th Regiment. He was the son of Aaron Kerley and Rebecca Alexander Kerley. His twin brother, Samuel Comodore Kerley, married Lewis' sister Harriet after the war.

Port Warlick was Portland Warlick, a younger brother to Lewis Warlick. He later became a 2nd Lieutenant in Company B, 11th Regiment N.C. Troops.

James Madison Gudger was a 2nd Lieutenant and later Captain in Company F, 4th Regiment from Buncombe County.

Zebulon Baird Vance, the first Captain, Company F, 4th Regiment, strongly supported the Union until Lincoln's call for troops. He quickly moved up to Colonel of the 26th Regiment. Vance had been a U.S. Congressman from Buncombe County before the war. He was twice elected governor of North Carolina, first during the Civil War and again after reconstruction. He also represented North Carolina in the U.S. Senate. His statue stands on the grounds of the State Capitol in Raleigh.

John S. McElroy was a Captain in Company C, 16th Regiment from Yancy County, North Carolina. He later became a Lieutenant Colonel, 16th Regiment.

Bob Patton's first wife was Lewis' older sister Elizabeth Emeline. She died in 1860. Harriet Warlick, a first cousin to both Elizabeth Emeline and Lewis, became Patton's second wife.

The railroad had been completed to within six miles of Morganton when the war began. The military companies Cornelia mentioned were marching to the railhead to board trains for Raleigh.

In Camps, Raleigh, N.C.
May 12th 1861

Dearest Cornelia,

Yours of the 6th Inst. came to hand day before yesterday which was read with feelings of gratification. You said you were afraid the next news you got from me that I would be on my way to Washington, well I can't say when I will get there but I can say to you that I will start in that direction in a few days, as we have been ordered by Gov. Ellis to proceed immediately to Richmond, in response to a call of Gov. Letcher of Va., he (Letcher) has made a call on the Gov. of this state for seven regiments forthwith.

I believe I wrote to you that we would be placed in the 2nd regiment, well when I wrote before that was the understanding but since that the 1st regiment has been disbanded and our company with the Buncombe Rifles were put in the 1st therefore, we will leave here sooner than I anticipated; the first reg. consists of ten companys about one thousand strong; we will be accompanied by the Fayetteville brass band to the scene of action. This band is said to be the best in the State. They gave us a splendid serenade a few nights since they played the National air of the confederate State (Dixie Land) which is a beautiful tune, it takes the place of Yankee Doodle and is sung by many soldiers in their humble camps.

I think Miss McCall did wrong by preventing her lover from going off to war; she ought have waited until he returned. You say there are more young ladies that would have done as she did provided, they had followed their inclination, perhaps there are, but I know that you would rather see your lover go off, than do as Miss McC. did; if you had have made such a proposition as she, it would have been very doubtful of my being here. I know I could not have rejected such an offer; What think you? If we had have got married last Winter which I was anxious to do I would not have left my "sweetie" under any considerations unless compelled by something more than honor.

My Dear, I wish I could be at Sardis Sunday, if I was there I know very well where I would get my dinner. I suppose you could guess. I hope the time is not far distant when we shall be permitted to meet again. The anticipation of that meeting makes my heart glow within me, should that ever come to pass I know that, that would be a time of unspeakable happiness. Don't you think so? But when I consider that we may never meet again it makes me feel sad and depressed to a great extent. I look at your type often and whenever I do it brings the past immediately to my imagination. The many, many happy hours we have spent together. You say to me not to forget my promise, i.e., to be a good boy   I will not, and will endeavor to conduct myself so as I will be respected by the whole company; and not only by them but by the friends I have left behind. Please write every mail, if you knew how glad I am to get a letter from you I know you would.

Your Lover

Direct as before.   Lewis

Margin Note: If you can't read this bring it to Raleigh and I will read it for you.

Margin Note: I forgot to tell you of the accident that happened yesterday. One of the Buncombe rifle men was accidentally shot in the left arm a pistol ball; it penetrated his arm about half way between the elbow and the hand and … but did break the bone; the ball has not been extracted yet. The wound is not serious, but will be some time before he gets over it.

Margin Note: My friend T. P. said he would write you a few lines, and asked if I would consent to putting it in my letter which I did.

Margin Note: One of the privates in the Randalsburg Riflemen from Mecklenburg shot his Capt. a few days since through the thigh, he intended killing him but was prevented by another man knocking down his hand at the time he shot, he is being tried today, but it is thought that he will be sentenced to death for an attempt of murder.

T.P. was Tom Parks. His letter follows.

Raleigh, NC
May 12th 1861

Miss L. C. & C. McGimsey's

    agreeable to promise I drop you a line. I have been well most of the time since I left. I have at this time a very bad cold & feel very badly therefore I cannot write as I would wish

a solders life is not a pleasant one I can assure you. Altho it is as good as I expected so far. I would much prefer being on Linville or Irish Creek to being in camp, but duty calls and I feel bound to obey. Camp life is quite different from being ones own master   I have only cross the lines three times since my arrival here   we drill about 4 hours a day and answer to our names 5 times a day. we shall leave here next week I expect, we are in the lst Regiment we elected our field officers yesterday. Hill Col. com.(*manding*)   Lane   Lt Col   Lee Maj

    I think from all I can learn that we will have some hard fighting to do & more over I am of belief we will be in it. Every thing goes on tolerable well so far. I feel my inability to write you a letter that will interest you   most of your acquaintances have enjoyed good health since and all in good spirits. I wish you to write to me & give me all the news. my best wishes to all etc. I will write again & try and do better, excuse my bad composition as I feel like anything but writing.

    Your Friend & well wisher

                Thomas Parkes

L.C. was Laura Cornelia, C. was her sister Celeste.

Thomas Parks later became a Lieutenant, Company B, 11th Regiment. He and Lewis were close friends during the war.

Colonel Hill was Daniel Harvey Hill, soon to become Brigadier General Hill.

Lt. Colonel Lane was James Henry Lane, an instructor at the North Carolina military Institute in Charlotte before the war.

Lee was Charles Cochrane Lee of South Carolina.

May the 19th/ 61

My dearest friend

I received your letter of the 12th Inst, and I assure you it was perused and reperused with the greatest pleasure. Sure enough my worst
fears are realized   you are going to Virginia   I have heard that the
first Reg. began to move yesterday to Richmond, and now I greatly
fear the next news will be that you are in battle, but I can only fear the
worst and hope and pray for the best; I see that old Abe said in one of
his public speeches that this war ended in subjugation or extermina-
tion of the South, I do not think that will ever be accomplished, I
think we have right and justice on our side; and that the God of Battles will protect us. What think you? My dear friend you said in your
letter that if I had complied with your request last winter you would
not have volunteered, I ask do you blame me for that now   I am sure
I did what I thought right, if I could have looked into the future perhaps I would have seen the error of my way, but I could not, and you
know whats done cannot be undone, no matter how much regretted; I
suffer from remorse of conscience   I know that I have said and done
a great many things that I ought not to have done, but will you not
forgive me? Oh! yes I know you will say freely forgive. — I hear that
Jacob Conly has returned home   I am very anxious to see him as I
suppose he can give the latest news from you all. I am very sorry to
have to inform you of the illness of Alpheus McGimseys wife   She
was very unwell when I wrote before, what I thought was caused from
cold   she has been getting worse ever since   three physicians have
examined her, and they all say she is taking consumption   She has always been one of my best friends, indeed she has been almost a
mother to me since the death of my own dear mother   I feel like I
can truly say that,
"Ever since childhoods happy hour
Ive seen my fondest hopes decay
I never loved a tree or flower
But twas first to fade away"
I know that we ought not to mummer at the dispensations of
Providence for we are afflicted for our good, but it is sometimes hard

to submit to them. Monday morning   I heard from Irish creek this morning   the folks are all well down there, Liz Parks and Jane Sisk sent word they were coming to Linville this week on a visit, I have not seen Jane or Hattie Warlick since you left. You ask me what had become of John Suddreth   I saw him at Sardis at preaching   I do not think he has much thought of going to war, as to Sue preventing him I believe she would rather he would go than to be branded with cowardice   I gave Sue her song ballad   She has learned to sing and play it   she sends her best respects to you and many thanks for the song Hattie Jewell sends her kindest regards and says she was glad to hear that you had not forgotten her   Puss says to give you her best respects and tell you to be a good boy. Tell Tom Parks that I had written to him before I received his letter but will write again soon   you must not neglect to write home you ought to write to your father. I believe I will be forced to quit for the want of something to write   I do wish I could think of something that would interest you, you write such good letters that I am ashamed of mine. Time will not permit me to write more now, please write soon   very soon to your devoted friend
Cornelia

excuse mistakes as I have written in a hurry

———•••••———

This letter is not in the McGimsey Papers. It is privately owned. A copy has been provided to the University of North Carolina, Chapel Hill.

Mary Ann Hunter McGimsey was the wife of Alpheus McGimsey, an older half brother to Cornelia. Alpheus McGimsey, Mary Ann McGimsey and their family lived in the same house with John Wakefield, Cornelia McGimsey and Celeste Ophelia McGimsey. Mary Ann died on June 5, 1863.

In Camps near Richmond Va
May 23rd 1861

Dearest Cornelia;

I have not received but one letter from you since I left home. Why is it? I would like very much to hear from you weekly. I have written you every week since I left with the exception of the last. We left Raleigh on the 21st Inst., and arrived here, in Camp, yesterday morning about 3. On our way to this place at every turn out and depot we were met by large crowds and especially by the ladies, who presented us with many boquets, cakes, etc. Richmond is a beautiful city it is splendidly layed of streets paved, and many superb buildings. I have to laugh at part of our company when they get into a city. They look at every thing and in every direction and their fingers pointed at every curiosity, which their eyes may behold; it shows at once they never traveled a great ways from their native place. There is now in the vicinity of Richmond about fifteen thousand troops. The 2nd regiment of Louisiana left this morning for Yorktown by orders from the Gen.

Our regiment (so says report) also two others from S. C. will leave for the above named place tomorrow. It is thought that, that place will be invaded shortly. Men women and children in this State are alive with excitement. Everybody is under arms and it seems they are anxious for the contest. It will be impossible for the enemy to entrap this State and keep their ground because the South has men that will defend their rights or die in the attempt. I think we have force strong enough to drive back a powerful enemy. There is now over a hundred thousand troops in the state ready to move at a moments warning to any place which they may be called to.

The city of Petersburg has sent out ten companys and are getting up two others; it is not who shall go to war but who it is will say at home. I was sorry to leave two of our company in Raleigh sick one of them was G. W. Anthony, he has Catarrhal Fever, he was left in the hospital; but one of our officers made arrangements before he left to have him taken to a private house where he will be well taken care of. Cornelia, it is only about a month since I saw you and it seems to me to have been a much longer time than that.

Often have I thought of the many happy hours we have spent in each others company; shall we be spared to meet again? I hope and trust we will, if that will be granted us. What a happy time that will be, it will be happiness beyond expression to make each other happy during life. I feel there is no one beside you who could confer upon me happiness and a peaceful life, any devotion for you will never change. it is fixed and firm and I hope yours for me is the same. Give my best wishes to Puss, Susan, Hattie and accept the largest portion for yourself.

Your Devoted Lover

Lewis

Margin note: Cornelia I wish you to write to me often   do not wait to get a letter from me to answer but sit down and write every week for you do not know how pleased I am to receive an espistle with your signature.

P. S. Direct to Richmond care Capt. C. M. Avery

Clark Moulton Avery was the company captain.

The Susan and Hattie mentioned here are Sue Moore who courted, but did not marry, John Suddreth; and Hattie Jewel, who corresponded with several gentlemen, including Lewis' brother Port Warlick. Lewis had two sisters named Susan and Harriet who are mentioned in other letters.

The nickname "Puss" is used for two different people. The most frequent reference is to Cornelia's younger sister Celeste Ophelia McGimsey. The other "Puss" is Cornelia's cousin Susan Elizabeth Alexander. Puss Alexander is always referred to with the last name Alexander.

The following letter was written by Samuel Erwin Penland. He was a mater-
nal second cousin and Cornelia's other beau. Cornelia's maternal grandmother
was Jean Penland Alexander. Sam Penland was in Vance's company when it
marched into Burke County on May 6th en route to Raleigh.

In Camp
Raleigh, NC
May 26th 1861

My Dear Cousin

    … Yesterday evening I was the happy recipient of a very interest-
ing and patriotic letter from you, at which, I confess I was much surprised. it brought the occurrences of a similar character to mind—
that you may understand to what cause I attribute that favor, I will
give you one that occurred in Buncombe—I have been opposed and
yet deny the right of secession (but not of revolution) consequently I
did all that I could in February to defeat N. W. Woodfin, the secession
candidate. he was defeated. Mortification and diabolical desire for re-
venge led him to denounce me and others, as others with myself finished like senior proclivities, as Black Republicans, he being a
gray-headed sinner we passed, and repassed as strangers until the day
we … when his cheeks blemished with hysterical tears, said, it was
time all party feelings and animosities should be forgotten and as
brothers be united in one common cause. The good of our country.
Then because I was willing to enlist in defense of my native state, the
rights and institutions of the "Sunny South" in general with those who
have been stigmatized and abandoned as submissionists and traitors;
while his allies or most of them lying supinely at home, he was to willing to take back all he had said and wish it to pass on terms of friendship; and now my dear cousin sentimentally am I not in part indebted
to the circumstances which summon us for your letter? Inferred from
your long silence that you thought me an unworthy correspondent. If
so then, I am not less so now. I did send you the Iredell Express, not to
elicit a correspondence or the resurrection of one that I thought forever entombed but simply because I wanted to give publicity to report that the Rough and Ready Guards were on the way to the tented
field, & knowing that you was a Lady of intelligence and refinement

you could appreciate the motions of those who have left kind friends and pleasant home behind to share a soldiers fare and meet a soldiers dangers. I have not written this to mortify you, but to justify myself— that the object I had in view may be, (and no doubt is) accomplished, and that the motions from which I was actuated may not be misconstrued. With all my heart I forgive, yes freely forgive you and extend friendships hand; thoughts of you have done anything for which, you ought to ask it, I do not know what it can be, as to responding to my letter, that was optionary with yourself: if I am wrong in regard to the cause, I can only implore forgiveness from one whose heart is ever open to the importunities of the petitions …

I think I sent cousin Rowan the next no. of the express, she will give you permission to read it. I wrote her have not received an answer. We have been here since Tuesday. A dispatch this morning says the enemy have taken Alexandria without resistance — that was in conformity to the orders of Gen Lee — to retreat and let them follow until they get out further from Washington. 25,000 are quartered there. Their Commander took the Southern flag down & Col. Jackson shot him. He died immediately. At a skirmish at Norfolk this week several vessels were badly damaged   Six of the men killed — nobody hurt on our side. Thus I hope it will ever be — I cant give news this time in conclusion if it is consistent with your wishes I know I will be glad to hear from you often and will make mine as interesting as circumstances will admit. In such times as these the light of christian example should be strong & steady. Our country is shrouded in thickest gloom   May God save our country from destructive war & prepare us all for the land of eternal felicity.

If you write direct to care Capt. Vance it will be forwarded if we are gone. Please excuse essay and bad writing.

Your Affectionate Cousin
S. E. Penland

In Camps Yorktown V.A.
May 29th 1861

Dear Cornelia

Yours of the 19th Inst. came to hand after days since which was gladly received and read with great complacency. You ask me if I blame you for not complying with my request last winter. Most assuredly I do not   I merely suggested the idea that it might be possible, I would not have been in the army, had it have been as I wished not blaming you in the least surely not. I have no doubt you considered it best for you to postpone the happy period; and I a man, not void of reason, was willing to acquiesce in your sentiments.

Cornelia, do not suppose for a moment, that I censure you in the least as regards doing rong; never oh never. I wish now I had not have written what I did, as it was calculated to produce uneasiness on your part. I would not say or do anything that would cast a shadow over your happy pathway, unless it was done through ignorance.

We left Raleigh the 21st Inst. and arrived at Richmond on the following morning. There we remained two days from thence to this point by way of railroad and steamboat, arriving here the 25th. Yorktown is situated on York river seven miles from Chesapeake bay. It is noted for being the place where Lord Cornwallis surrendered his sword to Gen. Washington. I have seen the very spot where that memorable act occurred it being marked with a monument to show to generations yet unborn where Washington achieved one of his greatest victories. His and that of the enemies trenches and fortifications many of them are yet standing; they are being repaired as for our protection. We are building a fortification around our encampment. Some of the companys are at work all the while day and night. On last Monday there was a dispatch received at headquarters stating the enemy were approaching by land; the long roll was sounded and in two minutes the regiment was in arms, we were marched in line of battle and ordered to hold which we did   expecting to see the enemy every minute; but further orders notified us they were not so near as first reported when we were dismissed with orders to be in readiness and be in line at a moments warning. Everybody seemed anxious for a fight.

The true statement of the fact, is, the enemy landed at Hamton on Chesapeake bay twenty four miles distant—nine thousand strong. Since Monday we have been looking for them day and night—and preparing to give them a warm reception when they do approach. Night before last our company was out on picket guard two miles from camp   we were placed in line along the road expecting every minute to see the enemy coming; day light found us standing there but no enemy. During the night there was a man fired at by Lieut. Dickson supposed to be a spy   he was hailed but made no halt taking to his heels when fired at. The river at this point is well guarded, there being a battery on each side mounted with the best guns some of them the famous Columbiards weighing nearly ten thousand pounds, carrying a ten inch ball. Lincoln's men-of-war can be seen in the Chesapeake every day. one of them approached within three miles a few days since when the battery on the opposite side of the river fired five shots at her thru taking effect the fire was returned but with no effect; the vessel went off disabled. We have about thirty five hundred troops here. Col. Hill says, the way we are fixed, we can whip five to one. At some of the fortifications where we have been at work, has been found human bones, powder, cartridges, bombshells, they are supposed to have been buried during the revolution. Write soon and often to your devoted friend and sincere lover.

Lewis

The following are notes written in the margins vertically and across the tops of the pages.

Do you wear our watch? If you do not I want you to wear it every place you go. I have not missed a Sabbath since I left home without hearing preaching. We have a chaplain with our regiment. This place suites me first rate as I can get plenty of oysters and fish. I go down to the river and eat oysters raw. I take them out of the shell and eat them without brew or anything else.

How is Mr. Wakefield getting along? What does he say about the war? Give him my respects

Direct all letters to Richmond, V. A. care Capt Avery, Co. G. 1st reg. N.C. Vol. I am some distance from Richmond but the reason I ask you to direct there is that the mail to this place is stopped, by directing there   they will be sent by special messenger to their destinations.

Give my kindest regards to Puss, say to her I would like very much to hear from her; also give my best respects to all the Linville girls.

I have a poor chance to write; but I have written to you every week since I left home with the exception of one.

The boys are well except H. Avery. He has been unwell for a few days but is getting better. My health is good.

———

Lewis Warlick's family had been Tories during the Revolutionary War. In Lincolnton, N.C. there is a plaque marking the spot where his great uncles, Nicholas Warlick and Philip Warlick are buried on the Ramseur's Mill Battlefield after being killed in battle on June 20, 1780, while fighting for the king. Cornelia's grandfather, Samuel Alexander and her uncle, John McGimsey, had also been at the Battle of Ramseur's Mill, fighting for American Independence and against the Warlicks. It is possible that Cornelia's relatives were responsible for the deaths of Lewis' relatives. Lewis probably had no knowledge of his family's Tory past when he wrote this letter.

The Confederate government always tried to link the rebellion with the Revolution. It was called the second war for independence. Jefferson Davis was inaugurated on Washington's birthday. North Carolina seceded on May 20, the anniversary of the Mecklenburg Declaration of Independence. When Lewis saw the relics of the revolution he could easily imagine he was part of a great patriotic endeavor.

Henry Harrison Avery was a second cousin to Captain Clark Moulton Avery. Harrison and his brothers and sisters were close friends of both Lewis and Cornelia.

Mr. Wakefield was John Wakefield. Lewis eventually began to refer to him as "Uncle John."

Linville River, NC.
June the 5th 61

My dear friend

    Last week I was the happy recipient of a very interesting letter
from you. I was very glad to hear of your safe arrival in Richmond, but
very sorry indeed to hear of your leaving so soon for the place of contemplated action, but perhaps it was as well to go soon as late although I know that you are now hourly expecting an attack, and it
may be have had one ere this, but it does not seem to me let come
what will that it can be much more than this awful state of anxiety
and suspense. You said that every body was alive with excitement in
Richmond   so they are here, some are almost frantic, I never hear
anything but war mentioned   I do hope it will not long continue
thus. I was very much surprised to hear that you had never received
but one letter from me I have written every week except one, I know
that our letters are detained somewhere, I never received but one letter
from you while you were in Raleigh. There was preaching at Sardis last
Sunday   the Irish creek girls were up, but I tell you there is a great
change, our seats that used to be crowded are now almost vacant;
some of the volunteers were up from Morganton   I believe Kirksey's
company intend leaving for Raleigh tomorrow. Mr Suddreth was at
preaching he attends regularly   I understand that he is very much
mortified about somethings that some of your company has written
back   Bill Hennessee told me that he thought he would go to see you
this week, I insisted on his going but I have not heard whether he
went or not   if he goes he will give you the news in full. Sue   Hattie
Puss and myself intend going to Irish creek tomorrow evening on a
visit   we expect to stay several days; for my part I do not anticipate
much pleasure; for while existing circumstances surround, enjoyment
is nowhere to be found by me. Lewis I often think of you and the
many happy hours we have spent together   if I could see you just one
hour I would think it a world of happiness, but alas! I fear I will not
soon realize it, if ever. Please write to me how your fare is   I know
you are nearly starved. Have you learned to drink coffee yet. I want to
know about the health of the place where you are, Tell Port and cousin

Bob I saw their types last Sunday   I think Ports is the most perfect
likeness I ever saw   cousin Bobs is not half as good looking as he
tell them the girls had like to eat them up, I think you ought to send
your type back as you have no very good one here   I would write
some more but it is so uncertain about you ever getting the letter   It
may be that before this letter reaches its destination you will be in battle   I trust it will not be so. May God incline his ear to our humble
petitions and may He save our country from destructive war and prepare us all for a land of eternal felicity   I will quit with the promise of
writing you a better letter next time.

as ever your friend
Cornelia

Please excuse errors and disconnection for I feel like any thing else but
writing.

—•◦•◦•—

*Elias Jackson Kirksey, a veteran of the Mexican War, organized a company
called the "Burke Tigers" in May, 1861. The company mustered in as Company E, 16th Regiment, N.C. Troops.*

*Cornelia's implication that God was supporting the Confederacy was preached
from pulpits throughout the south.*

*Cornelia has borrowed "land of eternal felicity" from Sam Penland's letter and
"I feel like anything else but writing" from Tom Parks' letter.*

In Camps, Yorktown, Va
June 11th, 1861

My dearest Friend,

Yours of the 5th Inst. was received this morning and perused with great pleasure. You do not know how glad I am to get a letter from old Burke, and especially from you.

I received a letter from you last week and would have answered it before this if I could have gotten paper and envelopes.

You say I ought to send my type home as I haven't any but poor ones, I would do so if I could get one taken but there is no chance in this place to get one, or anything else. It is a poor dilapidated place, although once the rival of New York.

I have been absent from this place since the 6th June. On that day we were ordered to march which we did, not knowing where we were going; none except the field officers; but before we got to our destination we heard that we were to pitch our tents at Bethel Church, which we did and went to work throwing up breastworks to be ready if the enemy should approach, we would give them a warm reception. We got there on the 6th and on the 4th there was four hundred Yankees there. We thought it might be possible we would find some of them there when we went but not so. Bethel Church is fifteen miles distant and nine miles from Hampton where there is a large body of Yankees. Hampton is two miles distant from Fortress Monroe and five miles from New Port News; at these three points there are thousands and thousands of the enemy.

Yesterday morning before day the long roll was sounded and the whole camp was in arms in three minutes; and soon was ordered to march, which we did, toward the enemy   after going three miles we heard the enemy was going to make an attack on Bethel Church that morning on all sides. After hearing that we marched back at quick time to our camp got breakfast, ordered to arms and awaited this approach til a few minutes before 10 when they came in sight; whenever they got in range of our field pieces they opened upon them with shells, which was returned speedily, bringing to … the infantry did not open upon the troops till they drew nearer. When they got near enough the rifles and musketry opened on each side with power, and continued two hours and a half. That was the hotest place ever I was in. The balls, grape, canister, and shell sung around us during the engagement tremendously. The enemy numbered forty five hundred (4500) and our force fifteen hundred (1500).

Although they had three to one, we came out victorious—gave them a gentiel whiping and sent them off running for life. The loss of the enemy is supposed to be between three and four hundred, the certainty is not known by us as they carried off their dead and wounded with the exception of fifteen or twenty. After the battle was over some of our men went on the ground occupied by the enemy and they report that they found any quantity of blood. From this and what we heard afterwards by some of the citizens, assured us they lost several hundred. The citizens say they carried off wagon loads of dead and wounded. Our loss was one killed and five wounded. I cannot see how it was that there was not scores of us killed. Surely the Lord was on our side. We were greatly protected by our breastworks, if it had not have been for them we would have been slaughtered by numbers.

I run a very narrow escape. I had the but of my gun shot off in my hands during the engagement. We left the battleground about dark yesterday evening and arrived here this morning at 1 o'clock; worried almost to death.

There is an attack anticipated at this place soon. If there should be and we whip them as easily as we did at Bethel, and I live to get home, I will be satisfied. It is a horrible sight to see men shot to pieces as they were yesterday.

If they had have kept out of the woods we would have killed many more.

I do hope we will have peace soon so we can return home to our friends and relatives.

I know that meeting will be one long to be remembered. Write often to your

Sincere Loving
Lewis

N. B. Direct as you have heretofore

The term "long roll" refers to a drum roll, which was a signal that battle was expected.

After this battle the men in other regiments began referring to the First N.C. Volunteer infantry as "The Bethel Regiment."

On July 6, Private Elam Bristol of Company G, "The Burke Rifles," wrote a description of the battle to his brother Billie at home in Burke County:

> ... The position assigned to Capt. Avery's company was rather in front of all the troops, the Captains orders from Col. Hill were when the enemy advanced upon us to retreat back across the creek (as we were on the opposite side of the creek from the rest of the forces) to a more secure breastwork. Which when the enemy came so near that we would have lost men had our Captain kept his men there. The order was given to retreat to the breastworks assigned for us which we did. . . . It is true the bullets whized all around us and come very near killing a great many of us (It was only by the Kind hand of Providence that all of us escaped alive). . . .

This letter is not in the McGimsey Papers. The complete text is in the Lambert A. Bristol and Elam B. Bristol Letters in the Burke County Library. Lewis mentioned Elam Bristol in several letters written in 1862.

This is a picture of the "Flag of Bethel" in the North Carolina Museum of History. This flag was made by the young ladies of Asheville from their silk dresses and presented to the "Buncombe Riflemen," a militia company which became Company E of the First North Carolina Volunteers. This flag was carried at Bethel and the word "Bethel" was sewn into the white stripe after the battle. After the First Regiment was mustered out of Confederate Service in 1861, the flag was returned to Buncombe County. Most of the men in the "Buncombe Riflemen" reenlisted in the 60th Regiment. Courtesy of the N.C. Division of Archives and History.

Yorktown Va.
June 16th '61

My dearest friend,

I this beautiful Sabbath morning have seized the present opportunity for the purpose of dropping you a few lines to let you know that I am yet in the land of the living. This morning, this beautiful Sabbath morning causes me to contemplate the past. The many happy hours I have spent in your presence and the many many hours of pleasure I have spent in the midst of my friends and relations. You say you did not get but one letter from me while I remained in Raleigh. I dont know how it happened for I have written to you every week since I left home, or except two, and will endeavor in the future to write as often as the times will admit. You wish to know how our fare is. I can say that it is very common, although it is as good as I expected when I left home. I knew before, that a soldier's life was a hard one, exposed to many hardships and severe trials, but a man should not look to that when his country is invaded with thieves and lawless persons, then every many should do all in his power for the protection of his much loved country and fireside. Since I left home I have gotten to drink coffee; but do not like it. Often we have hard ship biscuits and they are so hard, I have to soften them in coffee. This is said to be a healthy place. It is a summer resort for invalids; here we have the sea breezes every day, which is very pleasant.

Yorktown is one of the oldest places in America, and once the rival of New York; but now it is one of the most dilapidated places I ever saw. ... not excepted. Here stands a brick house, all the material of which was imported from England before the Revolution by Lord Nelson; This house at that time was the finest in the Colony. There can be seen several holes in the end which was penetrated by cannon balls during the engagement of Lord Cornwallis and Washington. We have this place tolerably well fortified. I suppose the whole of the embankments will exceed a mile. I think we can defend this place against four to one. At Bethel Church we held the place against more than four to one, and I know we are better prepared here for an attack than we were there. I have heard preaching every Sabbath since I left home.

Our Col. is liked by all the regiment; he is a cool deliberate man and more than that a christian, a strict member of the Presbyterian church. The Lieut. Col. is also a praying man. Our boys are in good health with few exceptions and all are in good spirits. They have been rejoicing considerably over their victory, and well they may for it was a glorious one. I wrote to you last week and tried to give you a description of it which was badly done. Give my kindest regards to Puss, Susan, Harriet and all my friends. Say to Mr. Wakefield I will give him all the news about war when I return.

Your devoted lover,
Lewis

Direct all letters to Richmond Care Capt. Avery Com. G 1st reg. N. C. V.

Margin Note: By directing to this place I can always get them. They will be forwarded to us no matter where we go.

Linville River, NC
June the 17th/61

My dearest friend

I received a letter from you last week bearing date May the 29th, it had been detained somewhere, but I assure you I was glad to receive it. I have heard since then that you have been in battle, and that you repulsed your enemy with a great loss of life and run them within two miles of Hampton. I hear that there was 4500 of the Yankees and but eleven hundred of our men and that Wyatt was the only man killed on our side, and none of Capt. Avery's men were hurt. If this statement is correct (and I suppose it is) ought we not to be very thankful for your success and the protection of your lines. Surely we are aided by a Higher Power. I believe success has attended our every effort yet, and my prayer is that it may thus continue. You no doubt have had another attack before this time, and I fear have had loss of life on our side, but I do hope you will be protected every time as in the first. The newspapers give all praise to the dear old north State and I have no doubt but that her brave sons merit it.

My dear friend I hope you will not in the hurry and amid the demoralizing influences of war, forget that our principal business is to "fight the good fight of faith and lay hold on eternal life." What a pity that man should die in a cause so noble, and yet without hope of endless life.

Perhaps a change of subject would be agreeable. I have been down on Irish creek visiting   went to see all my kin folks, I could tell you a good deal about my visit but I dont feel like it now, and besides we have all written about it. Puss, Hattie and myself, wrote to cousin Bob, last week. I suppose you will see the letter   I have written to you every week except two and then I wrote to your camp and of course expected you to see the letters. Uncle John has not been well for several days   he is getting better; you ask what he thought of the war and hard times; you know he is a poor comforter   he says he thinks the war will have a bad ending   let it end as it may, and that we will all be nearly starved, and the solders in particular. I expect you are most perished, but we have plenty to eat yet, we have currant, and cherry pies, beans and irish potatoes   we would gladly send you boxes of provisions if we thought you would ever get them. Will Avery called on us a few days ago   I would not be surprised if he was your brother when you come home I know he would like to be   he is courting Hattie, and writing to Liz Parks, I wish you would write to Liz and tell her so but dont tell her I said so; I heard from the creek this morning the folks are all well. Hattie Avery is on the creek this week   dont you wish you was there to take her home again   yes I know you do or rather I know I wish you were there   I will quit for I know I have written more than you will wish to read unless it was better   I never could write a letter in my life and now when I am about half crazy you know I cant

May God guide and protect and may you be able to subdue your enemy and return home safe and soon

is the wishes of your friend, Cornelia

It would be my highest pleasure to gratify your every wish, but I beg of you to excuse me for not complying with your last   I mean your watch   I would rather not wear it, I want you to come home and wear it your self   Corrie

Note: I have not been to Canoe hill yet   I have a thought of making you full fill your promise that is to take me down there if you ever get back and I trust you will come back soon.

Uncle John was John Wakefield, a much older stepbrother to Cornelia. He had been a soldier in the War of 1812. As a young man, John Wakefield fell in love with a girl whose family moved to Indiana. Following his heart, he traveled to Indiana and proposed marriage, but the girl rejected him. He returned to Burke County and remained a bachelor the rest of his life. John lived with the McGimsey family after his mother died, and continued to live with them after his stepfather Joseph L. McGimsey remarried Cornelia's mother. When Joseph L. McGimsey died Cornelia was only 12 years old, and it is obvious from these letters that the old man became a father figure to her and "Puss".

Private Henry Lawson Wyatt of Company A was the first Confederate soldier to die in battle in the war.

William Brown Avery was the son of James Avery and Elizabeth Brown Avery. His brother was H. Harrison Avery in the "Burke Rifles" with Lewis. At the time this letter was written he was courting Lewis' sister Harriet.

Yorktown Va,
June 23rd 61

My dear Cornelia,

Again I will attempt to write you a few lines although I am void of news. Everything in camps seems to be quiet; and has been for several days since Wednesday last. Then we had a surprise roll and every man in three minutes was under arms and marching to their designated places in the trenches where we remained for some time; until we ascertained it was all a false alarme.

The nature of the alarm was that the enemy was marching on the troops at Bethel Church, who were sent there on Sunday previous, twenty five hundred (2,500 strong) with a large force in front and a flank movement for the purpose of cutting them off from Yorktown. Col Magruder on learning which I have stated above from the picket ... ordered a retreat, which was executed immediately — they fell back to this place; but as I stated before it was all false.

I have understood that Col Hill was mortified by their retreating without a fight   if he had have been there with his regiment he would not have done so until he would have been obliged to do it, to save the lives of his men.

Col Hill has been promoted to Brigadier General, therefore we will have another Col. to elect.

Troops are pouring in here every day. if they still keep coming we will have a powerful army at this place, and well we may, for this is the key to Richmond & by which they intend going if they can; their whole aim is now to march to the heart of Virginia, to the Capital, but I doubt very much if he ever gets there; I know they will meet with some difficulty in passing this place.

There are a great many cases of measles in the army here, there are only three of our company who have them, one of them is Tom Moore. I heard through letters from home that you and the other Linville girls had been on a visit to Irish creek; I wish I had been with you, if I had gone I would have had some fun and perhaps a kiss which would have been worth far more than anything else in amusement.

I know Miss Neal if I had have been at home you would not have gone to see me, no you would have been afraid to do so and for what?

There was a serious matter occurred in our regiment a few days since; The Enfield Blues had some recruits from home and on the day of the alarm, there was one young man so badly frightened that he went deranged, and the next morning when the company was called out and the roll was being called, this young fellow picked up a gun and fired. The ball passing through one mans body and arm and through the arm of another, the first died almost instantly; his remains were sent home. On yesterday we lost another man from the regiment from sickness belonging to the Edgecomb Guards. There is less sickness in our company than any in the regiment. Some persons say we will be discharged at the expiration of six months as the regiment is only for six. We volunteered for twelve months, that is our com. And wether we will get off when the regiment does I cant tell. If I should get off I will go home, and if I should be wanted on I considered it my duty to enlist again after spending a few weeks at home. I will do so perhaps.

Your devoted friend

Lewis

Margin Note: Give my kindest regards to Puss and the rest of Linville girls. Oh how I would like to be on Linville today sitting by somebody perhaps you know who. How would you like that? I got a letter from Jane Sisk in which she said you were out to hear Mr. Carleton preach and that you looked so well; that much I always knew. I would like to be with you this summer to help eat some of Sid Conley's watermelons and peaches. I know he will keep you supplied in all kinds of nice things this season for he is clever. I have heard that "brother" Will and sister Harriet were pitching in very extensively, is it so?

Margin Note: I will have to quite from the fact that I have written up my paper and that it is nearly time for divine service.

———◆•••◆———

Miss Neal is a nickname for Cornelia

Colonel John B. Magruder was promoted to Major General after the fight at Bethel.

Jane Sisk was Lewis' niece. Her father was Bartlett Sisk and her mother was Lewis' older sister, Catherine Selima Warlick Sisk.

Pleasant Hill, NC
July the 4th, 1861

My dear Friend,

I once more seat myself to drop you a few lines in answer to your
two last letters; I would have written you last week, but was on the
puny list with a <u>bad</u> cold and neglected to write. I was very sorry to
hear that you had measles in your company   I think I have heard you
say that you had them; but I know there is several in your company
that has not. I fear you will have a great deal of sickness in the army
this summer; I hope you will use every precaution, and not expose
yourself any more than you can possibly help. You no doubt was surprised to see so many new recruits with Brown and McDowell   I
hope you received them all kindly, and extended friendships hand, regardless of the past; I suppose they have given you all of the news from
Burke   Did you get your letter? I did not know that John Suddreth
and Sid Conley were going to join you when I wrote. Now you see I
will not get those Water melons.—It is rumored here that the confederate troops have taken Alexandria and Washington city; but I fear it is
too good news to be true;   there is so much news afloat now that I
cannot believe any thing I hear until it is authenticated. You said you
knew if you had been at home I would not have gone to see you, I
dont know whether I would or not; but you come back and I will tell
you what I will do. I think you have grown very distant to address me
with 'Miss. surely you had forgotten who you were writing too   You
said it was thought that you would get off at six months   that seems
like a long time, I hope we will have peace before that time. If we do
not I know there will be many lives lost, and here let me beg of you, if
you do not value your own life for my sake do not expose yourself to
danger when you can avoid it. I was sorry to hear that you had to elect
a new Col. You sounded to be so well pleased with Col Hill.
Your brother Will and sister Hattie are flying round extensively he is
<u>taking on</u> considerably, whether he is progressing very fast or not I can
not say. — Liz Parks has accused me of writing something about her,
but I will not acknowledge it, just to tease her. There is preaching at
Sardis next Sunday   O! how I wish you all could be there; but Alas!

Who knows but that you may be in battle. Hattie Jewell and I are speaking of going to Canoe creek on a visit next week & if I get well of my cold, but I believe it gets worse instead of better. I think it approximately a <u>distemper</u>. The Linville folks are all well so far as my knowledge extends, accept sister Mary A. McGimsey. She improves very slowly if she improves at all. Tell John Suddreth I think he might left "good-bye" for a body. Puss says she will answer your letter next time I write as she has so many to answer this time that she cant answer yours. Tell cousin Bob I will invite him next week if <u>nothing</u> <u>happens</u>. one request write soon and dont forget to

your devoted friend
Cornelia

I received a letter from Camp Bragg last week and tell you it was infatuation I never was flattered in all my life <u>afore</u> it made me blush to read it   he insisted that I should write often to my sweetheart if he was in the army. I wont tell you who it was from but you may guess if you can
C

Have you observed the comet   I look at it every night and wonder if you are not looking at it too

———•◦•◦•———

Calvin Scott Brown was 1st Lt.

2nd Lt. James Charles Sheffield McDowell was the grandson of Revolutionary War Colonel Charles McDowell.

After the war, Harriet Warlick married Samuel Commodore Kerley, a twin brother to Cousin Bob Kerley.

The comet Tebbutt was first spotted May 13, 1861. By summer it was very bright and easily seen in North America.

Yorktown, Va.,
July 6th, '61

My dearest friend,

As I have an opportunity of sending a letter by hand to Morganton, I concluded I would write to you although I haven't any news, but believing you would like to get a line from your absent friend at any time, for this reason I am now writing. I wrote you on the 2nd in the morning in which I stated that Lient. McDowel and recruits had not arrived. They arrived that evening and you cannot imagine the rejoicing there was over them. We were all pleased to see them and among them were my friends Sid Conley and John Suddreth to my great surprise.

How did John get away from Linville. I know it was a hard trial, from experience. Susan will undoubtedly get all the war news in the future from her "most-loved one".

Tom and I got the cheese you sent us. You do not know how proud I was of it — to think that I had a friend among the fair sex of old Burke who thought enough of me to send at a distance of five hundred miles something that we poor soldiers could eat — a thousand thanks to you for it, and a long life of pure happiness is my sincere wish.

Our company all got cakes, ham etc. from old Burke which they devoured with a good appetite after eating bad bread and salt meat. Out of some bodys box of provisions there was found a letter directed to me. It was handed to me by some of the boys, which I opened and at the bottom of the fourth page I found the name "Cornelia" which caused a thrill of joy to pop over my whole frame.

You wished to know of me if ever I thought of going home, on a visit; well I can say in regard to that, that I tried to get off when McDowel left but did not succeed in the attempt.

As for private or non commissioned getting a furlough to go home; that its almost an impossibility, unless depressed of health. You say everything that Jane Sisk wrote me was true, I do not believe it. She said she had seen you at Sardis at some time and that you were almost crazy about me, how I would believe that.

You know as well as I that she was jesting. I am glad to hear that the ladies have resolved not to marry until the volunteers return home.

I would not be surprised if marriage licenses would advance in the price then. I think it would be well enough for me to send on for mine now and reserve them until I go home for fear the <u>Clerk</u> will sell out before I can get into the office. What do you think about it? You wanted to know how I managed about cooking, washing etc— whether I am ... As for cooking and washing I don't have any of that to do; our mess has a cook hired who does all our work when well.

Last week he had the measles and we had to pitch in and do the cooking ourselves, which went against the "grain" considerably. I have had to much to do that I have not had time to write to Susan. Today I have been out cutting down timber about a mile from the quarters so as we can see the Yankees at a long distance.

————•••••————

There is no signature on this letter, but the handwriting is Lewis'.

Yorktown, Va
July 18th '61

My dearest Cornelia,

Yours of the 4th Inst. came to hand yesterday which was received and read with much gratification.

I was sorry to hear that you were suffering with a cold as you were not able to answer any letters as I am always so anxious to hear from you. If you know the feelings of delight that come over me when I open a letter and see your signature at the bottom of the page; I know you would write at least every week not every day but every three days.

You asked of me if I did not value my own life for your sake not to expose myself to danger when I could avoid it.

Let me say to you that I think more of my existence than anyone else and will not throw myself in the jaws of death on purpose to have my lamp extinguished, far from it, I desire to live a long life of happiness with my darling beauty I left behind.

It is you that will cause one to quit the army sooner than anything else. If I had not a sweetheart in old Burke I would see the end of this war in the service of my country battling for the rights which we will have; provided I did not loose my life in some of the struggles.

You said that you had a letter from Camp Bragg from some man and wanted me to guess who. Well as to guess who he was would be an impossibility as I do not know where the place is. O; yes, I can tell you now it was your old beau J. C. B. was it not? I like his persuasion very well as to you writing often to your beau in the army, I want you to take his advice as I consider it a good one as good as I could give.

We have yet several cases of measles in the hospital, among them are H. H. Avery & Sid Wakefield. They are getting better in fact all are doing very well except Bill Powell. I heard a few minutes ago that it was very doubtful about his getting well, he was well enough to go about at one time, but could not be kept from running about so much that he took a relapse and very likely to kill him. As yet we haven't lost any men, some of the company's has lost three or four from sickness and accidents. All in camps is quite — no news of a battle soon, although we may hear of the enemy advancing before night. It is distressing to the citizens of the Peninsula, the Yankees have ruined them forever, they have taken all their property negros included   they have even gone into the houses and stolen the women's and children's clothing, broke pianos, side boards and every thing that could be found in a rich mans parlor. I heard a minister of the gospel from Hampton last night say that the loss of Elizabeth City county would exceed half a million of dollars.

There was an old gentleman here a few days since, who said twenty thousand dollars would not pay his loss by the rascals. Hampton numbered eighteen hundred inhabitants, all have been forced away except a few families of poor people.

You cannot imagine the destruction they have had to bear.

Your Lover Lewis

Margin Note: Say to Miss Hattie that Port is a candidate for county court clerk and that she ought to use her influence for him in order to secure his election. J. R. says he has not written to ... yet but will do so soon   he is well and in good spirits. Give my best regards to the widow Suddreth and say to her I will take care of her old man as long as I stay with him. Give sister Puss and all the rest of the girls my best respects. Miss Hattie Avery's beau is in our regiment Mr. ... perhaps you have heard of him, he belongs to the Southern Stars, he is a nice clever fellow. Write often to your loving friend in the army.

Lewis

The "Southern Stars" from Lincoln County mustered into the First N.C. Volunteers as Company K.

Pleasant Hill, N.C. July 25th 1861

My dear, dear Friend,

Day before yesterday I returned home from Canoe creek, Hattie
Jewell and I went down to Canoe Hill Last Friday evening. We
stopped at Theodore's, and Matilda Roderick went with us; when we
arrived at Mr. Averys we found Puss and Laura Alexander there and to
our great joy the old folks were not at home. There was eight girls, and
not a gentleman on the place if we didn't have some fun Oh! Hush …
Hattie Jewell and Puss Alexander were the life of the crowd. Hattie
first acted like one of the old South mountain women come to <u>town</u>
to sell eggs, berries, etc. She said her husband had gone to the war, and
she was left alone she seemed to be in great distress, about him; but
while she was talking who should step in but her husband home from
the war. Such a meeting and so much joy I never saw you cant imagine
how they did take on. Hattie then went out and put on Mr. Avery's
coat, hat and a mustache, of soot. She came in and introduced herself
as Mr. Port Warlick just from Yorktown, you ought to seen us rejoicing over him,   We soon began to interrogate him about those left behind we ask if you ever said anything about the girls in the camp. She
said no that you did not care a red cent for any of us and that you had
all sort of fun over our letters, she said some rich things about you
sure, but time will not permit me to tell you all. I think it would take
about a week to tell you all that was said. You know I could never
write it. I was afraid to look at the carpet next morning I expected to
see it threadbare; but as luck would have it there was no holes in it. Liz
Parks and Jane Sisk came down Saturday evening we all stayed at uncle
Bobs that night, I cant tell you what all we did Saturday night, suffice
it to say we had a fine time. Hattie Jewell came home Sunday her
<u>Sweetheart</u> from S. C. (Mr. Nichols) came up Saturday and of course
she had to go home with him. Tell Port he had better keep awake and
write fast or Mr. Nichols will slay him. I dont want him to do that for
I would hate so much for Hattie to go back to S. Carolina. Will Avery
came out to uncle Bobs to call on us Sunday   you know it is a treat to
have a gentleman call on a lady <u>now</u> <u>a</u> <u>days</u> for they are as scarce as
beggars dimes. Will kept me posted in news while I was down there

and I have come to the conclusion that he is right clever after all. What think you? — Laura Avery had a beau while I was down there. I suppose you have seen him. The Rev. Mr Mason I think he is very nice and very polite indeed. Aunt Sophie requested me to give you her best wishes and kind regards and to tell you that she was fattening a pig and raising a heap of chickens   said she intended to give her friends and relatives a big dinner when they come home from the war.

Since I commenced writing I received a letter from you dated July 18th. You cant imagine how glad I was to see it   I was getting uneasy about you as I had not heard from you for a few days you are not as well pleased to receive a letter from me, as I am to get one from you I know, if you could see me taking on when I get a letter from you you would think me crazy sure enough. You are not good at guessing   J C B sends all his letters to the post office he is an ardent admirer of Miss Hatties   Camp Bragg is near Sufflolk Va   my letter was from one of my Buncombe friends who belong to Capt. Vances company. Tell John Suddreth if he dont treat Sue better I intend to scratch him off my book   I know he could have written her ere this   I dont suppose he cares a straw for my friendship, but I might say something in his favor   Sue told me she didnt intend to write to him until she received a letter from him. I heard Hattie Avery speaking of Mr. Haynes when I was there I think she said he had measles the last she heard from him   I was sorry to hear of H Avery and S Wakefield being in the hospital   I do hope they will get well soon it seems like Harrison is unfortunate this is two spells of sickness he has had. I will tell Hattie that Port is a candidate for County Court clerk she surely will exert her influence in his behalf I fear he will not be elected as so many seems to be tied to Kincaid he did not announce himself soon enough! We have heard of a hard and bloody battle at Manassas Junction great loss of life on both sides the confederates whipped the Yankees and run them to Hampton   It is stated that our men got their big cannon   the loss, on our side is over five thousand   Col Fisher was killed and nearly all his Regmt   there is not enough left to form one complete Company   Jo and Sam Brown belonged to that Regt and many others from about here. Surely old Abe will see that he never can subjugate the South. I do hope they will be compelled to acknowledge the independence of the Southern Confederacy soon, and that we may conquer a speedy peace. I believe it is about three months now since you left Morganton surely it has been the longest three months that ever was; it seems to me to have been six and just to think you cant come home for three months more, who knows, but before that time you may be killed   I know we ought to be very thankful that your lives have been spared, while so many have fallen in Battle   Surely the Lord will have mercy upon us; and avert the dire calamity   I hope He will incline his ear to our humble petitions and save us from destructive war. Suppose I turn over and change the subject.

We have had very little sickness in our neighborhood this summer Mr James Hunter is sick now he has been confined about a week   I do not know whether he has fever or not, as he has not sent for a physician yet. I think Mary Ann McGimseys health is improving some, but very slowly. Have you ever been sick since you left home. I know that you never have written to me that you had been sick; does your weak eye ever pain you now, I was fearful it would hurt your eyes to be exposed to the sun so much. I have heard you say that you had weak eyes. What have you done with my old ugly type you surely have not kept it all this time   I know if I had been you, I would have disposed of the ugly thing long ago   How many in camp have you showed it too? I know even one that would look at it is it not so. Uncle John has gone fishing this evening and will not come back tonight   Puss and I will have to stay by ourselves unless some one comes to stay with us. We are great soldiers not afraid to stay alone but I am inclined to think we are like most braggarts the greatest solders in time of peace. I expect you will be sadly disappointed when you see this letter, you will think you are getting some news of interest; but it all amounts to very little, judging you by myself I thought you would be pleased to hear any thing that comes from Burke. You gentlemen will not condescend to write such simple things as we silly girls do. You will not write any thing short of a battle or somebody being sick or killed. I assure you the most simple thing that occurs in your camp would be interesting to me. Your letter is before me now the only fault I can find with it there is not enough of it; but do not trouble yourself for my gratification. I am very glad to receive a letter from you regardless of length. Laura Avery told me that she was going to write to Port and give him the news. I suppose she will keep him well posted in the news and times in Burke. We all wrote to Charly McGimsey from Canoe Hill. Tell him he must answer every one that wrote to him   I thought I would finish out this page, but I fear you will be wearied before you get this much read and I concluded to not write any more this time. Please <u>do</u> <u>do</u> <u>do</u> write soon and often

to your unchanging friend
Cornelia

Will Avery was later a sergeant in Company F, 41st Regiment, N.C. Troops

Uncle Bob was Robert Alexander; Aunt Sophie was his wife.

Laura Avery was Will and Harrison Avery's sister.

S. Wakefield was Sidney Daniel Wakefield. His uncle was John Wakefield (Uncle John) and his father, William Wakefield, was Cornelia's other, much older stepbrother.

Cornelia's second cousin Sam Penland wrote the following letter.

Camp Ellis, Suffolk, Va.
July 28th 1861

Dear Cousin Corrie

Think not that delay has been voluntary, for I assure you an immediate response, but for the intervention of circumstances over which I had no control, would have been given ... —I have not Brother here, three of them belong to a company that has not left Asheville—one is at a Theological Seminary in N York City and can't get away. another and the last, eleven years of age is at home, the youngest that has volunteered is Sixteen. T.J. Candler, a second cousin is here and several others more distant   James M. Gudger is our second Lient. I have not seen him for a week, he is sick and in the hospital though not dangerous. The health of the fourth is good with the exception of measles and three or four cases of typhoid fever. Corrie you ought to pray often, (and I know you do), for one is already answered—"a ... breese has sprung up and give a settled turn" to several thousand Yankees; their first grand march was to the field of carnage and death at Manassas and there in glorious retreat was back to Alexandria and Washington. Scott and Lincoln were there with many Congressmen to celebrate the victory, they did so by leaving their carriages & taking a more expeditious way of traveling to save themselves—they were so sure of victory that an account of the battle and their success was published in the New York Herald the very day it was fought giving the plan of attack together with the Regts engaged.—the plan of attack was the same they tried to carry out but with what success you have already doubtless seen. What a strange dream yours was but I believe it will be realized before Lincoln subjugates the South. It will be a pleasure to me, to comply with your request, but I have to wait til I go see the Artist which will be next week if we remain here. I would like to know what sort of a looking personage your imagination has pictured. Won't you give a description before you receive it. Your happiness was marred by not realizing your dream—that you may not be disappointed again, let me prepare you.

I resemble the Erwins more than the Alexanders   Look out for <u>yellow hair</u>, eyes and skin of the same color features anything but presupposing. Well I cannot give you any idea?—don't you wish I wouldn't send it.

I enclose a piece for Cousin Rowan, please hand to her. My respectful compliments to your kind sister Goodbye til you write again to your ever affectionate cousin.

(no time to correct ...)   S. E. Penland

———•••••———

Winfield Scott was Commanding General of the Army. General Scott and President Lincoln were in Washington during the battle.

Cousin Rowan was Rowena Kerley, a sister to Bob Kerley.

Private George Phifer Erwin wrote the following letter on the same date Sam Penland wrote to Cornelia. He and Samuel Erwin Penland were distantly related. Phifer was valedictorian of the class of 1861 at Davidson College. Immediately following his graduation, he joined the "Burke Rifles" to serve with his cousin Clark Moulton Avery, the company Captain. His mention of "cousin Moulton" is a reference to Captain Avery. This letter is not in the McGimsey Papers. The complete letter is in the George Phifer Erwin Papers at the Southern Historical Collection, Wilson Library, U.N.C. The letters in this collection may not be used without permission from Southern Historical Collection. A typed copy of this letter is in the Burke County Library.

Yorktown, Va.
July 28, 1861

Dear Mother,

I Received your last letter a couple of days ago and also a short note from Pa. I was truly rejoiced to hear of Aunt Kate's improved health and I am now under no apprehension as to her final recovery....

... Cousin Moulton has been around to see me, but none of the other officers of our company. That was, I presume because I was not really sick and because measles are so common that no one pays any attention scarcely to them....

... I hope your fears on account of our reverses in western Virginia have been cast away by the news of Beauregard's victory. There are now 1200 prisoners in Richmond and some 6 or 800 more at Manassas. These are the unwounded, how many the wounded are I cannot say. They, the unwounded, are all together in some large tobacco warehouses in Richmond and strange to relate, some New York merchants who have many independent fortunes from the tobacco trade of Richmond, are now prisoners of war in the very houses of which, but a short time ago they were the customers and out of which they made so much money. War causes many strange incidents in many a man's history. They have also caught several of Lincoln's congressmen. One name I know—Eli—from New York, who voted so strongly for millions of men & millions of money to aid in conquering us.

One of the prisoners said to a gentleman, that the only word of truth he had heard from his commanding officers, was when they told him that he would be in Richmond in July and there he was, sure enough though not in the manner looked for. The papers come much nearer the truth this time than I have ever known them, probably because the results of this battle are so large that the sensation editors consider no enlargement necessary.

The report of 30,000 handcuffs and any quantity of nooses prepared by the Yankees for our benefit and captured, is all true. Their plain was to surround Richmond immediately after they defeated us at Manassas and prevent the escape of our Congressmen. They were to be handcuffed and sent to Washington. And the Yankees intended having a triumphal procession after the regular old Roman style. How they could succeed in capturing our Congressmen even had they defeated us at Manassas is a mystery to me, but let a Yankee alone for laying large plans. 61 pieces of artillery were taken by us for certain—there may be more—So certain were they of getting to Richmond that the boxes had on them the names of the places in the city where they were to be stationed. Some were marked Capitol Square others Shocks Warehouse, & in fact everything was prepared for their encampment in the city & marked to the different places to avoid any confusion.

Sherman's Battery, one of the finest of Old Abe's was taken by Fisher's Regiment, but I don't believe they will ever get the credit of it. Fisher first ordered his men to kill all the horses so that it was impossible for the enemy to get the cannon off when they retreated; when that was done, they took it at the bayonet's point. Fisher being on foot & leading the charge. He ordered Coz Isaac to hold it—while he (Fisher) was so excited and so pugnatious that he rushed on sword in hand, some thirty or fourty yards in front of his command. (I do not think he had the whole Regt. with him at the time and then it was when he was killed. His body was borne off immediately.) A Regt. of Ala. Troops seeing this party there & supposing them to be Yankees fired into them. Coz Isaac knowing them to be Confederates of course could not return fire but, as the best thing, ordered his men to fall back. The Alabamians rushed up and planted their colors by it. This is the account I have had from very excellent authority and I have no doubt as to its correctness. I have not heard how it has been decided only I saw in yesterday's papers that there were several aspirants for that honor—but even there, Fisher's name was not mentioned. These Virginia papers will not do us North Carolinians justice.

It is also true that Scott was on the ground and it is also true that his Carriage, sword and epaulettes were captured.

These few incidents of the battle I have given you hoping they may prove interesting for, even if you have seen them in the papers, there is some satisfaction in knowing that there is some truth in them. That was a glorious victory and will open the eyes of the northern populace, because the results are too extensive and too palpably evident to be escaped or avoided. The prisoners at Richmond say they've had enough of war and if they were at home Lincoln and his party might go somewhere else for his fighting material. It will have an immensely cooling effect on the northern mind....

... The enemy here on this Peninsula have entirely destroyed Hampton—burned it yesterday and it has caused a good deal of speculation here. Some think that they intend to blow up Old Point and abandon us entirely and throw the entire force into Washington. Others think they will abandon all other points except Fortress Monroe leave a small force there and carry all their possible force to Washington. We believe Old Scott will find great difficulty in equipping another such army as he had at Manassas. For that one was splendidly equipped,— however much we question its courage....

... Tell Pa not to trouble himself about a horse for me.

Give my love to all—to Aunt Kate, Coz Julia, Uncle Hamp, Aunts Tilda & Mary and everybody else.

Love to Pa, Sister & Sallie and much love to yourself.

Your devoted son,
G. P. Erwin

P.S. Tell Nancy Ed is well and is very well satisfied. He wants to see her very much but is willing to stay here with me. He sends love to her and all his friends and howdy to all of you.

—•◦•—

Cousin Isaac was Isaac Erwin Avery. He was the Captain of Company E in the Sixth Regiment (Colonel Fisher's) and later became Colonel of the Regiment. Isaac was a brother to Captain C. Moulton Avery.

Ed was a servant with Phifer for three and one half years of the war. Phifer mentioned Ed in almost every letter he wrote to his family. Nancy was Ed's love interest back home.

Neither Sam Penland nor Phifer Erwin was at Manassas.

Isaac Erwin Avery. Courtesy of the N.C. Division of Archives and History.

Pleasant Hill
July 31, 1861

Dear Friend,

Being alone to day and having an opportunity to send you a letter I could not refrain from dropping you a few lines but I will tell you now in the commencement that I have not one thing to write only that I am well and hoping these few lines may find you enjoying the same like … I wrote to you last week and wrote every thing I could think of, but as you say you would be pleased to hear from me every three days I will write whether I write any thing or not. The folks on Linville are thrashing their wheat out now. I think their crops are turning out tolerably well   uncle John had his wheat thrashed yesterday   I think we will have plenty of cake to eat and enough to spare you a biscuit or two if you'll come up; and judging from the dark green color of the corn I think we will have some corn bread too perhaps   Ned could get a few grains of that provided you was with him. I believe tomorrow is the election; well I suppose I will have to vote for my Brother   I do hope he will be elected there seems to be a great change since his announcement   I told Hattie what you said   she says she has got several votes, and if she could have got a horse to ride she would have rode round a treated for him   I understand that Will Avery is spreading himself for Port but I fear his influence is like my own not very great. Sue is going to vote for my brother and I am going to vote for hers. I mean Sid Suddreth (enough of this)   I think I told you last week that Mary Ann McGimseys health was improving. Last Monday morning she was taken suddenly sick   She was very sick for a while we did not think she would live   we sent for the Doctor   he came and relieved her   the doctor says this spell of sickness has nothing to do with her disease   She is better now   I think she will get able to walk about again, but I have no idea she will ever be well   Puss is with her now. Mr. Hunter is but very little better   the doctor says he has fever.

I would write more but Theodore McGimsey is waiting for me to finish and take my letter   I am going to send it in Charleys and Bill's box of provisions   one request   write soon and dont forget to

ever your friend
Cornelia

Mr. Hunter was James Hunter, a son of Andrew Hunter and Lydia Burchfield Hunter. He died in 1863. He was an uncle to Mary Ann Hunter McGimsey.

Theodore McGimsey was a son of Alphonso Joseph McGimsey, Cornelia's other half brother. Although Theodore McGimsey was Cornelia's nephew, he was actually older than she. Bill McGimsey and Charlie McGimsey, privates in Company G with Lewis Warlick, were Theodore's brothers. Theodore joined the 58th Regiment in 1862 and rose through the ranks from private to Lieutenant while fighting the Yankees in Georgia, Tennessee, and North Carolina. "My brother" probably refers to Alphonso Joseph McGimsey.

Pleasant Hill, Burke County, N.C., as it appeared in 1998.

Yorktown, Va
Aug 3rd '61

Dearest Cornelia:

Yours of the 25th Inst. came to hand yesterday which was opened
and perused with great haste. You say that Aunt Sophie is fattening a
pig and raising a great many chickens for the purpose of giving her
friends and relatives a big dinner when they return from the war. I am
glad to learn that she is making such extensive preparations, and especially her relations will be counted among that number. I hope if that
be the case that I will be a participant at that anticipated feast—What
think you? I consider Aunt Sophie a very patriotic lady as ladies are in
general.

My eyes have not been sore but very little since I left home; some
times when I take cold they hurt me slightly. My health generally has
been good since I left home—have had but little sickness.

You want to know what I have done with your "ugly" type. I can
say to you that I have it yet but badly abused as I have been comparing
it to some others boys sweethearts' types, and am happy to inform you
that it is prettier than any I have seen. Now are you mad? I told you a
story   I have not compared it to others, but have shown it to some of
my friends. I know you dont care how many I show it to so far from
home. Well what do you want to know now? You say that you want
long letters—that we will not write anything short of a battle & c—
that anything from the camp would interest you the same way it is with
us. We like to hear anything from old Burke, we would run any distance to see the meanest dog in old Burke if we knew he was in camps.

Gen. Magruder ordered all the force from his place yesterday except this regiment; besides them he got a large force from Williams-
burg, Jamestown and Grove Wharf, and is gone in the direction of
Newport News; various rumors are afloat as to his intentions, some
think he has gone to attack Newport News and some think differently.
I would not be surprised to hear cannonading in that direction before
tomorrow night.

If there is any chance to get a fight he will get it as soon as any
man, for he is brave & daring—cares not for any numbers. I suppose

his force will amount to ten thousand. It is rumored in camps that Gen. Hill, as soon as he gets well, is going to make application to the President to be sent to Manassas; but I think it is as a great many other reports—false. Report says the intention of sending us there is that it is to avoid this sickness that we have, as there is a great number of our regiment sick. We report about three hundred and seventy (370) sick including officers nearly one third of our number. Mart Marler and C. McGimsey is sick and gone up the river to a country hospital—dont think they are dangerious. H. Avery is very sick and considered dangerous; he has got a discharge from the army with the intentions of going home; but now he is entirely to weak to undertake the trip and I understand now that the officers are going to send him to the hospital where Mart and Charley are.

Capt. Avery and Lieut. McDowel are confined to their beds. The Capt has fever and ague. All the other neighbors boys are well or getting well. H. Galloway, Will Corpening, S. Wakefield and others are walking about and beginning to look well. Mr. ... as you heard has not had the measles is looking well and goes to see H occasionally.

Our cook has left and gone home and we have to do our own cooking as we have not been able to get another. This week I have been deprived of drill, cooking and every thing but laziness with a boil on my foot that pained me greatly—it is getting better. The best cooks in the mess are T. Parks & Omark and some say I cook tolerable well but I dont like to own to it as they will want me to do a good chance of the work over the fire, and you very well know that I haven't any great thirst for labor of any kind.

You would laugh to see the boys kneading dough, they do it very awkwardly and bake some of the worst bread you ever saw—other things general poorly prepared as we have not the right kind of cooking utensils, and more than that we haven't the "wherewith" to cook nor the ingredients to go in it.

Mr. Armfield has got a discharge from the army on account of bad health, and will start home on Monday next. If you see him he will give you a general history of a camp life—better than I will attempt to describe it to you on paper. I was at the Capts quarters yesterday looking at a map of Va.—looking out the different places where there had battles been fought & c, when I looked around, my eyes beheld two ladies approaching. I kept my eyes on them until they advanced near enough—I tipped my cap—bowed politely—they inquired if that was Capt. Avery's tent—I replied it was they said they wished to see him and at that time Joe Kincaid bounced from his seat and ushered them in the presence of the Capt. and Lieut.; after talking to them for some time they retired and I with many others stood there like fools looking at "heavens best gifts" to man and why did we do so? Because ladies visits here are like angels "few and far between."

One of them was Lieut. Col. Lee's lady who had arrived the day before from Charlotte, the other one I didn't find out who she was, and didn't care particularly about knowing her as she was "homely" and you know I never did care much for an ugly woman; unless I was well acquainted with her and knew she was kind, interesting in conversation & c. I am waiting anxiously for the next month to come so I can go to eating oysters again; at this season they are not healthy. We are beginning to live better; we get cabbage potatoes & other vegetables by buying them—the government does not furnish anything of this kind, all we get from it is meat, flour, meal, rice, soap, sugar, coffee and candles sometimes peas, not often.

I suppose you know we will be sent home at the expiration of six months. I know you will be all mad about it as you have had such a fine time while we have been absent from old Burke—have had no boys to trouble you—you girls could do as you pleased—almost whip a fellow if he didn't do right and there was not one to take his part—make them do as you wished. Isn't it so?

The Chaplain (Ed) Yates has returned from the old North State where he was gone to recruit his health. I have learned through the papers that none of our acquaintances were killed in Fisher's regiment, only fifteen were killed and seven mortally wounded. It was almost a miracle that there was not more of them killed as they were right in front of the celebrated Shermans battery, the best in the U. S. and made a charge—drove off the union, all who were not killed, with the bayonet and took the battery.

Your lover

Lewis

Magruder was Major General John B. Magruder.

Companies D and E of the 6th Regiment had many Burke County residents. Isaac Erwin Avery, Capt. Clark M. Avery's brother, was the first Captain of Company E. Samuel McDowell Tate was the first Captain of Company D.

Fisher was Colonel Charles Frederick Fisher, 6th Regiment, N.C. Troops. He was killed at first Manassas, July 21, 1861. Fisher had been president of the North Carolina Railroad before the war. When the war broke out in 1861, the railroad had been completed from Salisbury to within six miles of Morganton. After Fisher was appointed a Colonel and work was halted on the railroad, many of his railroad work crew joined the 6th because they wanted to fight with Fisher. Fort Fisher, at the entrance to the Cape Fear River near Wilmington, is named for him.

Linville River, NC
Aug 21st 1861

My Dear Friend,

As some time has elapsed since I heard from you, I have concluded to write you again thinking that perhaps you did not receive my last letter. I think you ought to have written before this whether you received my letter or not   why is it that you have not written? You must know that I am anxious to hear from you often particularly when I hear of so much sickness at Yorktown. I hear that Mr. Corpening has returned home; but I have not seen him   I was sure you would send letters by him, but we sent down there, and didnt get any. I was at the burial of Harrison Avery   his death has cast a gloom over our community   his was the first death in the company, but who knows whether it will be the last or not. Harrison was a nice clever boy I always esteemed him highly as a friend   truly "death loves a shining mark."   I do deeply sympathize with his parents and relatives, in their sore bereavement; but they sorrow not as those who have no hope   I doubt not he has gone where sickness and sorrow, pain and death, are felt and feared no more, and where the shock of battle and the conflict of contending armies will never again disturb his peaceful rest. I hope you all went to see him often during his sickness. There is no telling the distress that this war has caused in our land—Oh! that some propitious breeze would spring up and give our affairs a settled turn. I do hope and pray that "He who maketh wars to erase unto the end of the earth" will speedily cause the dark raven of war to plume her dusky wings and take her flight to the land of terrors from whence she came. — I must hasten on for time waits not for delay. The Nebo camp meeting comes off the last of this week. Oh! what a change since the last camp meeting there   perhaps you remember something about it   I am not going to attend for how could I enjoy myself when I would think so much of the absent ones. — Mr. Higgins and Miss Ann Eliza Conley were married yesterday   they intend starting to Florida soon on account of his ill health. There is some sickness in Burke now   Sallie Fendley died a few days ago   Mr. Hunter is sick yet   he improves very slowly   Mary Ann McGimsey is able to walk about   I cannot see much change in her. I have heard of a battle being fought recently in Missouri   reports say the federalist were repelled with considerable slaughter also that Gen. Lyon was killed. I have not learned the particulars as we have not sent to Morganton this week for our paper. I saw Mr. Armfield at the burial   he was so sunburnt I hardly recognized him   if you are all his color I think you would do very well to ship South   I did not see him but a few minutes and then there was so many talking to him   I barely spoke to him. — We have during the last four or five days had a super abundance of rain. I do hope the copious showers may cease descending for a while. Please do write often   I tell you if you dont answer my letters I will quit writing unless you have some better reason than I now know of. If you get sick you must get a furlough and come home. Puss sends her respectful compliments to you and says to tell you she thinks you have treated her letter with silent contempt. In conclusion I insist on you writing soon to

your ever affectionate friend
Cornelia

———◦◆◦———

Mr. Armfield was Mark Armfield, a corporal in Company G, First Regiment North Carolina Volunteers. He was promoted to 2nd Lieutenant in October. Lewis was incorrect when he wrote Armfield had been discharged. Mark Armfield became the first captain of Company B, 11th Regiment N.C. Troops. He was captured at Gettysburg and died while a prisoner of war at Johnson's Island, Ohio.

The Nebo Camp Meeting was a Methodist Revival usually lasting about five days. Nebo is in McDowell County about 10 miles from the Linville River.

This letter was written by Celeste Ophelia McGimsey, Cornelia's sister "Puss."
She refers to Cornelia as "Neal."

Linville River, NC
Aug 29, 1861

Kind Friend;

I accept this early opportunity of responding to your kind letter which has come to hand at last   it had been detained somewhere for more than a week. Think they ought to have sent it sooner and not caused so much unnecessary grumbling and uneasiness. I believe I am going to find myself in the fix a great many folks do when they want to write but nothing to write. There was considerable disappointment on Linville last week on account of no letters from Yorktown   I tell you I was rather uneasy about Sue and Neal was almost sure I would have to send for a physician   I rendered them all the assistance I could but it all seemed not to avail anything   I believe they are better now and look as if they thought I wont care for any one that dont care for me.

Sue and I intend going to Canoe creek tomorrow if the weather is not too inclement   Mr. James Avery has been sick ever since Harrison was buried   all the family took it very hard but they morn not as those that have no hope   I was very sorry to hear of Harrison's death. Company "G" is deprived of one of its brightest stars truly "death rides on every laping breeze and lurks in every flower." I was rejoiced to hear of our great victory in Missouri achieved by Gen. McCoullock but sorry to hear of so many souls being ushered into eternity and per-haps unprepared but they would have it   so we are not to blame   I am expecting to hear of Washington City being attacked every day am anxious to hear the result   Oh! that the dark gloom of war that is now gathered over our country would disperse and give us peace again. I have understood that France is going to help the North but have not heard it confirmed   I want France to stay at home and mind her own business and not be dabbling in things that dont concern her I suppose they think they will subjugate us and then take our cotton Perhaps they wont succeed   If they dont I hope the South will not let them have cotton enough to cover a chiggers head;   You say you heard I was kicked and asked if it was so. That was one of Neals white stories   if I have been kicked it dont have the same effect on me as I heard some say it had on them   I think she (Neal) has been kicked or something ails her from the way she sighs and groans   if you dont hurry and come back her nose will be growed plum down over her chin and you know she looks none to well at her best.

Alpheus McGimsey has just come in   he says tell you he has been out hunting an killed a big deer   he is as proud of it as if he had killed a Yankee. You say you get water melons plenty   I do not think you ought to eat them   they are the worst things you can eat for chills and fever   do use every precaution and guard against sickness if possible. Neal is going to answer your long communication   I suppose I had better stop and not weary your patience any more with my scribbling

> "May heavens richest blessings decend on thee
> And when life's streams are o're
> May it throw a sacred pearl be cast
> On God's blissful shore."
>> Dont forget to write your friend
>> C. O. McGimsey

⸻•✦•⸻

General Ben McCoulloch, formerly of the Texas Rangers, commanding a Confederate army in Arkansas defeated General Nathaniel Lyon at Wilson Creek, Missouri, August 10, 1861. General Lyon died in battle.

"Squire" James Avery was born in Warwick County, Virginia, very near the place of Harrison's death. James' father, the Episcopal Reverend Isaac Avery, had been a minister at Bethel Church and had held prayer meetings on the grounds which later became a battlefield. When the Reverend Avery died, his son, James and two of his daughters moved to Burke County, N.C. to live with their Uncle Waightstill Avery.

Ships Point Va
Aug. 31st '61

Dearest Cornelia

Yours of the 21st came to hand last evening for the first in about three weeks. I had supposed you had forgotten me altogether. You cannot imagine how glad I was to get a letter from you, if you could have seen with what rapidity it was opened you would doubtless been surprised.

I was astonished to hear that you got no letters by Mr. Corpening, for he carried a letter to sister Puss from me; he must have lost it or he would have sent it to her, he had a great many letters and it may have been misplaced.

You say that Mr. Armfield was so sunburnt that you scarcely recognized him, he is a fair specimen of the Company in general, we are all sunburnt if you could see me I know you would not claim me for a … I have not shaved since I left home and look savage—look like a civilized being would run at my approach from fear. I was sick when I last wrote you and have been until a few days since in fact   I am not stout yet have not been on any duty.

I had chills and fever   I tell you they pulled me down in a hurry, I do hope I will have no more for they make a person feel awfully mean and very sick at times.

The health of our company is improving slowly and I think as the cold weather approaches it will continue to improve. Ship Point is at the mouth of Pocasin river on a small bay leading into the Chesapeake. In front of us is the bay. on our right the river and on the left is Cheesurns creek; our camp in a beautiful grove of pines where we can get a sea breeze all the while.

This place is said to be a healthy location and some think it is for that that we were moved here in order to recruit our health which is very essential, and probably while we are here we can induce old Wool to come out of Fortress Monroe and give us an attack, if he comes we will try and give him as good as we gave Butler.

We heard exciting news from the Old North State last evening. It was that Gen. Butler had sailed with his fleet to Fort Hatteras, attacked the place, whiped them out, took them prisoners and took possession of the place which is all true I suppose   as I see it published in the Petersburg Express. When we heard it every man was anxious to strike tents and go at once and whip them out. Our officers say we can on our own soil whip ten thousand for we whiped five thousand on Va soil and they know we can whip twice the number on our own, and more than that they are the very fellows we whiped at Bethel and we want to get another trial at them. Our officers are now getting up a petition, petitioning the War Department to send us there, there will be some doubt about it being granted. You say if I dont answer you will quit writing. Im sure I write more than you. Please write often to your best friend

Lewis

Margin Note: We will be disbanded on the 13th Nov then I suppose we will all go home to see our sweethearts and friends. I expect to get married when I get home if I can get any one to have me   if not I will go into the army again in about three weeks. What do you say to a matrimonial union next fall? I hope to find you all ready for that long to be remembered day when I get home.

Margin Note: Say to Puss I have answered all her letters. Give her my kindest regards.

—•••••—

Old Wool refers to Union Major General John E. Wool.

Major General Benjamin Franklin Butler had sent Union troops to attack the Confederates at Bethel Church. In late August he was in command of a joint army and naval attack on Confederate forts at Hatteras Island. This victory on August 28, 1861 gave a tremendous boost to the Union morale. After losses at Bethel, Manassas, and in Missouri, the Union was beginning to believe the rebel boast that southerners were better fighters. This was the first real northern victory. Hatteras Island also provided a base for the Union to conduct future operations in eastern North Carolina. In May of 1862, Butler commanded land forces in the capture of New Orleans. He was the Military Governor of New Orleans from May, 1862 to December, 1862. In 1863 he returned to the eastern theater of operations.

Camp Fayetteville, VA
Sept 11th '61

Dearest Cornelia

Your note by the Captain came to hand a few days since which was gladly received though short. It found me suffering with a severe fever as I had had a shaking chill a few hours previous, which is the last I have had and I hope it will be the last so long as I am in Va; that was on Sunday   I had one the day before.

I had the chills checked on me at Ship Point and I was imprudent enough a few days after to go out on an expedition for the purpose of blowing up or burning up a lighthouse 6 miles above Fortress Monroe, we started about three hours before sundown (twenty three in all) in small boats and was gone the whole night, did not return until daylight the next morning, was traveling all the time, had no way of lying down to rest being exposed all the while to the night air that was I believe what brought the chills back upon me.

After all our trouble and danger to which we were exposed we succeeded only in part, which was that we arrested the light-house keeper and brought him prisoner to Ship Point; the light-house we could not burn nor could we blow it up as it is solid masonry from the base for forty feet. Therefore we had to leave that fine piece of property to benefit on by the Yankees who plough the rough billows of Hampton Roads with their freighted ships men-of-war, etc.

This is the reason we wanted to destroy it as it is of no use to us at all now, for we have no ships upon the bay and if we had, the great navy of the North would soon capture the last one. They (the Yankees) are greatly helped by that light to guide them along the channels and roads at night. They would have missed it very much if we only could have destroyed it, but failing to do so we heaved a sigh, set sail and rejoiced only over the capture of our man who was sent to Yorktown from Ship Point to stand a trial for being a traitor which I suppose he is as he visited Fortress Monroe often and received pay from the Lincoln Government for keeping up the lights. That shows he was not true to his country.

We keep moving, we only remained at Ships Point two weeks and then we were ordered here for what purpose I cant tell. We are now six miles from Yorktown, in a pine grove and have the best water we have had since we have been in Va., and for that one thing I would like to remain here until our time expires, if we could get to stay here I think we would all get good health again. I got the cheese you sent me for which I am very thankful. The socks I have not got yet but Bob says he will give them to me at any time and for those I am under many obligations to the donor and wish her long and happy life.

I understand that Sid Conley has got a discharge from the army and will start home tomorrow   it was on account of bad health.

Several more in the company ought to be sent home as they will not do any good while we stay here on account of their inability. Say to sister I will answer her letter as soon as possible. Write soon and often to your best friend and something else

Lewis

━•❖•━

Backriver Lighthouse was six miles above Fortress Monroe. It was built in 1829 and was functional until 1936. The lighthouse was reduced to a pile of rubble by a hurricane in 1956.

Cornelia's cousin Robert Kerley went on the lighthouse expedition and sent Cornelia a letter the same day Lewis sent his letter. The complete text of this letter is in the McGimsey Papers.

Camp Fayetteville
Sept. 11th '61

My cousin Cornelia,

I am gratified with the opportunity of responding to the kind and affectionate letter which came to hand through Capt. Avery, … We left Ship Point on the 3rd day of Sept, we left for the purpose of taking some prisoners and burning a lighthouse, which was used for guiding their vessels from sea. Our three little boats were ready and we started about 4 o'clock…we sailed on until dark overtook us about 10 miles from Ship Point in sight of 6 of Lincoln's war vessels. … we could see their lights onboard plainly … we reached the lighthouse expecting to arrest a host of Yankees, but was dark … no Yankees except the old man who fixed the light.

We set the lighthouse on fire leaving about 5 pounds of powder in it to burst the mason work, all for nothing. We left in quick time you may guess fearing the…. might send their Cavalry in pursuit of us as we were in 4 miles of Fortress Monroe. We shortly reached our boats and returned to Sailors for Ship Point…the gale was so high that our boats run aground….

… Take good care of your dear self, … write soon to your absent

Cousin Bob

Camp Fayetteville, Va
Sept 15th 1861

Dearest Cornelia,

Again I will endeavor to write you a few lines although I have but a short time to do so as I want to send this by G. B.(*yron*) Kibler and he is going to start in a short time! If I had have known last night in time that he was going to leave so soon this morning I would have written then. He is going home on furlough to see his sick father who is very ill and not expected to live. I suppose he will give you all the camp, war, and all kinds of news, he was the best pleased man when he started home I every saw.

I am glad that I can say that I am getting about again; I went out on drill yesterday for the first time since I left Yorktown and I tell you Col. Lee put us through in a hurry. Gen. Hill has returned with his health very much improved. I hope our regiment will be placed in his brigade for I consider him one of the best commanders in the Peninsula and one who our regiment would follow further than any man in the service; you may consider what great confidence we put in him.

Lieut. Col. Lane is going to leave us as he has been elected Col. of the 3rd regiment, the Col. of that regiment being appointed to the command of Fishers.

We dislike very much to loose Col. Lane as he is one of the finest men in the service and more than that we cant get a man in the regiment capable of filling that position, and we cant get a good man outside who will be willing to come in for two months only.

Our regiment has been presented with a very fine flag by the ladies of Fayetteville, among several inscriptions on it is the word "Bethel" in large letters. Among other things connected with it is that I have been appointed one of the color guard to protect that flag in time of battle, if the color bearer should be shot down it is my duty to seize the colors and again let them flout to the breeze, and so on if I should be shot another of the guard has to take hold and never let it be out of sight of the men who fight under it. I guess you will say that the Col. made a bad selection when he chose me for that position — that the flag would be badly protected if we should get into another engagement dont you? Mr. Armfield speaks very highly of you among other things that he said, was that you were very pretty. I will be compelled to quit as Byron is going to start now in a few minutes.

Write often to your friend and ardent lover

Lewis

Tell Puss I will answer her letter some time this week. Give her my respects.   L

———•••••———

Camp Fayetteville was named to honor the ladies of Fayetteville, N.C., who made the regimental flag. This flag was carried until the end of the war and never surrendered.

This is the design of the North Carolina State Flag adopted by the Legislature on June 22, 1861. The date May 20, 1775 was the date of the Mecklenburg Declaration of Independence and the date May 20, 1861 was the date North Carolina seceded from the Union. The obvious attempt was to link the war of rebellion with the Revolution for Independence. The Bethel Regiment Flag had the word "Bethel" inscribed on the white bar. According to Lewis there were other inscriptions. At Appomattox, the officers of the regiment burned the regimental flag rather than surrender it.

Pleasant Hill, NC
Sep 19th 1861

My Dearest Friend,

This morning I received a letter from you (brought by Mr. Kibler) telling me the good good news that you were getting well again. Oh! you cant imagine how glad I am to receive letters from you, — when it is such a pleasure to receive a letter from you what would it be to meet you, — to see you safe home again — I leave the answer to some other mode of expression than the combination of words or the computation of numbers. You said to me that you would join the army again in three weeks after you returned home, you must not say that   how can you think of maring the happiness of our meeting with the thought of parting again so soon you must come home and stay through the winter, and then if you have to go back next spring I am going with you provided you would let me   I am sure I do not think any hardship could be much worse than the anxiety and uneasiness I have suffered with since you left. You said something to me about your imprudence going to burn a light house causing you to have chills again   I do not think any of your acted either prudently or wisely. Lieut. Brown says he never expected to see one of you again when you started. I dont think you deserve any praise for rushing into danger uncalled for. How often will I have to beg you for my sake not to expose yourself to danger, but what is it worth my while to plead with you to take care of yourself for you will not listen to anything I say. Oh! the unutterable anguish that heart must endure — which lavishes all its best affections on a creature mutable and perishable as itself, from whom a thousand accidents may separate or estrange it, and from whom death must one day divide it. Yet it is only time and suffering that can teach us to comprehend the miseries that wait on the excess even of our virtuous inclinations   I feel that I am due you an apology for not writing sooner. I went to a quarterly meeting at McDowell's Chapel last Sunday   did not get home until Monday when I received your letter sent by Sid Conley   I went over to Mr. Rutherfords Monday morning, and did not get back until last night after dark. Laura Avery, Puss Alexander, Sue Moore, and myself, were a delegation sent over to Mr. Rutherfords to ask a donation of him for our Soldiers Aid Association   how we succeeded we promised not to tell suffice it to say we were paid for our trip. Now I must tell you about our adventure going over there   Sue dropped her vail in the road we all tried to pick it up with our switches but could not and Sue had to get down for we had no gallant. She led her horse up to a stump on the road side and was just going to get on when a yellow jacket stung her   she stopped to see what was the matter by this time they were swarming round her horse   it soon began to cut up all sorts   pulled loose from Sue and came very near running over her   took off through the woods as fast as it could run so there we were   Sue frightened almost to death   it was all we could do to keep her from fainting   she was as white as cotton. I tell you she shouted once if she never does again   tell John Sudderth he ought to have been (a)long to see how pretty Sue looked—I think she looked like and angel   her face pale, her hair falling round her shoulders, the tears rolling down her cheeks, clapping her hands and hollering. I cant give you any idea how strange she did look. Puss Alexander said that Laura and I must stay with Sue and she would go in pursuit of the horse   she sprung up on her horse out of the middle of the road for she was afraid to go to a stump and went in a hurry after going about a half mile she saw the horse standing in the road—she jumped off hers ran up to Sues horse and caught it   we started to meet her but soon heard her coming on her way rejoicing   I think it was a fortunate circumstance after all   Sue might have been thrown and killed and John Suddreth left a widower. Good luck to him. Our kind old friend did not let us come back alone   he sent a servant with us. We met up with Sid Conley at Mr. Gillwoods as we came home   he said he came up on purpose to see us   I think he looks a great deal older than he did when he went away no wonder he was glad to start home   he looks like he had seen hardtimes   he walks lame yet and cant use one arm   he told me you looked well   I know you never looked any other way. You said in one letter if I could see you now I would not claim you for a beau   well if I did not you would have to change in some other way except looks. Austin Parks was here today   I suppose you have heard that he was a volunteer in a cavalry company   B. H. Sisk is a volunteer in the same com(*pany*) Aus told me that Pink Warlick wanted to volunteer but your Father would not consent   I dont think there will be a young man left here until you come home. Allen Conley and Charley Parks say they will volunteer — Saturday they elect their officers. I believe Dr. Ellis has his company very near made up   I do wish I had time to finish this sheet but uncle Barnet is waiting to take my letter and I must quit. I dont believe you will ever read half I have written   I could not spell anything this evening   I believe I am about half crazy any way   Puss says to tell you she is going to make a home made dress hopes she will get it done to receive you in when you come home I ask you to burn this letter when you read it and if you cant read it burn it any how. So please write often to

Your unchanging friend
Cornelia

Margin Note: I am very sorry to have to tell you that our Father would not give us one cent for our association   dont you think he ought   we meet again next Wednesday   Good bye dearest one.

Margin Note: Was your socks large enough   I would send you the proceeding of our first meeting but Laura Avery said she sent it to Port.

———•••———

John Rutherford was one of the wealthiest men in Burke County. He lived at Bridgewater Plantation.

"Our Father" probably refers to Lewis' father.

B.H. (Bartlett) Sisk was Lewis' brother-in-law. He was in the 3rd N.C. Cavalry for one year. This regiment later became the 41st Regiment N.C. Troops.

Dr. James R. Ellis of Hickory Tavern was Captain of Company K, 35th Regiment, N.C. Troops. He was also the Company surgeon.

Pinkney Warlick was a younger brother to Lewis and Port.

Austin Lenore Parks and Charles Benjamin Parks were younger brothers to Tom Parks.

"The Soldiers Aid Society of Burke County" was a formal organization of ladies who met each Wednesday at ten o'clock in Mrs. Walton's parlor (which Mrs. Walton wasn't specified, but it was probably the wife of Col. Thomas George Walton). Officers were Mrs. Corinna M. Avery, President; Mrs. Minerva Caldwell (wife of the future Governor Tod R. Caldwell), Treasurer; and Miss Ann E. Pearson, Secretary. Ladies were asked to solicit money and cloth, arrange to cut cloth and make garments, and assist in packing boxes. The secretary maintained records of contributions and noted which companies received boxes. Mrs. Corrina Morehead Avery was the daughter of former Governor John M. Morehead and the wife of William Waightstill Avery. William W. Avery was a Confederate Congressman and the brother of Captains Clark Moulton Avery and Isaac Erwin Avery.

Linville River, NC
Oct 4th / 61

My Dear Friend,

There is so little transpiring here that one finds it almost an impossibility to frame anything like a respectable letter. Our Soldiers Aid Society met again to day   there was a great many ladies and but two gentlemen there. We boxed up what clothes we had made and intend starting them to Kirkseys company in a few days   we had forty shirts, thirty one pairs of drawers, eleven towels, and one hundred pairs of socks. I have just returned home and Liz Parks came home with me. Liz and Puss are talking so much and telling me to write so many things that will not do to write that I cant write anything. Liz Parks can tell as big stories as ever   She has a new dress and a new black silk fixin trimed with green (I dont know what the name of it is)   She says she had been dressed in satin seventeen days, to go to Catawba but got disappointed as usual   she says she cried so much that she raised Irish creek with her tears till it over flowed the bottom   Liz says she has cried and pulled her nose so much because none of the boys wont write love talk to her that she can touch it with her toes when she walks. Dont you think thats a whopper? I guess you have understood that Allen Conley has volunteered. Puss has cried so much about him that her eyes are as red as big Almonds and her face ten degrees longer than usual. What do think of this? Hattie Jewell is enjoying herself finely   I think she is raised to the forty seventh heaven   Tell Port Jo Brown is at home and if he dont hurry and come home there will be no chance for a dutchman at the post office. Sue Moore got a letter the other day. She kissed it and took on over it terribly before opening it and low and behold when she did open it — it wasnt from her dear John. Liz and Puss have talked out I believe and gone to eating apples   the candle gives such dim light I cant see the lines. I guess I have written more than you will wish to read. In conclusion I insist on your writing soon to

your true friend
Cornelia

———•••———

Liz Parks was Tom Parks' sister.

Following is a letter written by Cornelia's sister, Celeste Ophelia written on the back page of Cornelia's letter to Lewis. "Neal" is a nickname she uses for Cornelia.

Mr. Lewis

So Neal has poured out any amount of fibs and says she cannot possibly fill this poor little sheet of paper to her lord and master. She says I must finish this sheet. I am sure if it was me writing to an absent lover I could fill a sheet as large as the <u>New York Day Book</u>   But the reason I guess is I am present and she cannot give loose to her pen for fear I might speak out in … Do you know Neal has got another man's likeness beside yours? Well she has   She brought yours and the other mans out for me to look at and I kissed the other mans and just puckered up my mouth to kiss yours and she give me such a lick on the head I dont think I will get rid of the jar before Christmas. We have been disputing about which one is the best looking, she says yours is, I say the other mans. So you see we cant agree. She has kissed your likeness til it is as greasy as fat …, if she keeps on it will be so dim in a short time she will have nothing to look at but case and glass. Neal has been inquiring around to see if some one could form some plan to keep you here when you come home, some one has suggested to make a rope and tie you to the bench, she has six cuts to spurr and if she can get six more … against you come home   she thinks she will have a line strong enough to hold you but she thinks it will take a strong one to hold you for you are a buster   Neal has told you about our clothing we gave to send to the volunteers   I will tell you about a pair of drawers made in Powelltown under one of Hattie Averys apprentices, they are about one and a half yards long in the seat, and are cut eight cornered before and large enough in the waist for Dunn Kincaid, the seams are filled in ridges about the size of a halter and nothing under the sun to keep them over the hips. I'll bet the man that gets them will curse sight. I wrote to you last week. Hurry and come home or Neal will go into spasms. I will have to stop any scribbling as Neal is preparing to retire and we have all kinds of terrible work with   the candle has been out three times. As ever your friend   you know who

---

The New York Day Book *was a newspaper.*

The other man's likeness was that of Samuel Erwin Penland.

Camp Fayetteville York Co. Va.
Oct. 7th 1861

Dearest Cornelia,

Would you like to hear from me again? Well what do you want to read? If you were here and tell me what you wanted to know probably I could write something that would interest you, but without I cannot. The most I think of now is that the time of our disbandonment is fast approaching and that we will be permitted to go home (Providence providing) and see our friends and relations. Will not that be a joyful time? I know it will be with me and many others. The thoughts of you and I meeting is a source of great pleasure, and this I have not language to express myself in regard to that meeting. It will be joy unspeakable and the anticipation of that memorable meeting   being so near at hand is the beauty of it.

I wrote you some time since that I expected to reenlist in a short time after I returned home, which was all true; but since that time I have concluded not to go into the army until next spring. Part as I will have to stay at home after this as father is getting old and there is no one there now to attend to his business since the death of Mr. Gill. If Port goes into the army next spring I will be necessarily compelled to remain at home unless my country should make a call for all to aid in the defense of her rights and institutions, then it will become every mans duty to adhere at once and march against the enemy of our beloved country and put them to flight as at Manassas.

If I was to go into the service this fall, I have not a doubt but that I could get a Lieutenancy which would be but little if any inducement for me to enlist, for it is neither honor nor money that would lead me into the cause; nothing but patriotism. There is some talk of reorganizing the 1st regiment in a month or two after it is disbanded, which I hope will be done, for it is considered one of the best in the field and I would like to see it keep up and retain its reputation throughout the entire war. I dont speak well of it because I belong to the 1st, but because Virginians, Georgians and all others speak of the 1st N. C. V. as being men who will not shrink from any duty that is assigned them, and Virginians in particular say there is more morality attached to the 1st N.C. than any regiment on the Peninsula.

Jason Conley, David Branch and Bob Conley are very low with typhoid fever. Jace and Dave are improving, but as for Bob he is the only one who has Typhoid fever in the company. Port has chills again also several others, and as for myself I am happy that I can say that I am as well as I have been since I left Raleigh. The impression still prevails that Gen. Magruder is going to attack Fort Monroe. The movement of the troops and the preparations making look very much like it; there are now at Yorktown a number of scaling ladders and report says there will be several hundred of them sent to this regiment to practice the boys in running up and down them so they will be able to scale the walls of a fort with great agility. As for myself I dont care anything about the exercise for my cowardice would prevent me from ever facing the point of a bayonet on a fort ready to receive my heart's blood; the thoughts of which is enough to chill the blood that flows through the veins of the bravest of the brave. If it was not for the country's good that we are fighting for, we never could stand the smoke of the battle and the roar of the cannon as we do; but so long as this war continues Southern hearts will not quail, never no never.

You have asked me several times not to rush into danger, to expose myself where there was not call for it. You need not be alarmed for my want of courage will always keep me from running into danger unless duty calls on me to go into danger and then if I can, I will do all in my power to accomplish the end which is pointed out not shrinking from the contemplated consequences. Is not that right? If I did not perform the duties assigned me it would be far better for me to be at home engaged in something else.

I am anticipating a fine trip to Catawba and Lincoln after I get home on a visit to our relations with you as a consort. Will you go? I feel inclined to believe that you will; and if such be the case J. L. W. be as happy as I cant tell.

I wrote to sister and enclosed in Tom's letter. Say to her that I want her to make haste and finish her dress in side of six weeks for by that time I expect to visit Pleasant Hill. Say to Susan that her <u>old</u>

<u>man</u> is well and the same in camp as at home; he complains that she does not write to him. Give her, Puss and all the girls my kindest regards.

Your unchanging
Lover
Lewis

———•••••———

R.S. Gill was a wagon maker who lived with the Warlick family until his death in 1861.

Lincoln County and Catawba County are adjacent to Burke County. Johann Daniel Warlick, the common ancestor of all the Warlicks, immigrated to America in1729, and settled in Lincoln County about 1750. He began operating a mill which survived Indian attacks, the Revolutionary War, and natural calamities until 1949, when it was finally dismantled.

Yorktown Va
Oct. 25th '61

Dearest friend,

Again we are at old Yorktown. We left Camp Rains on the 20th
for Bethel where we remained until yesterday. On yesterday at three A.
M. we were aroused from our slumber and ordered to march at once
to this place, that the enemy was landing on York river in large numbers three miles from this place and if we did not march immediately
leaving baggage that in all probability we would be cut off; another
order soon after was that we should take all the baggage we could so
we went at once to striking tents and packing up to load the wagons
which we did in short order and sent them on to this place, the regiment remaining behind until the wagons returned to camp for the second load then every thing was put in, the regiment order to "fall in"
and "forward march" was given at two P. M., we came on in high spirits expecting that it would be the last move we make until we left for
home, but alas! We had not proceeded but three miles when the Col.
received an order from Gen. Magruder to return to camp; halted and
rested until the Col. went to Gen Rains head quarters and told him
that he had received orders from the Gen. in command for the regiment to return to Bethel and further told him that all the baggage had
been sent to this place, Gen. Rains replied to come on   the Col. went
back and started the Reg. immediately to their expected destination
the men were so well pleased they gave a tremendous shout. We arrived here last night at dark. The report of the Yankees landing on
York river was all false. We are now under marching orders to return
to Bethel today, but I understand Col. Lee has gone to head quarters
to try and get Magruder to let us remain here until tomorrow as we
are all very tired, I dont know how he will succeed. I am tired of so
much moving. I wish we could get to stay here during the balance of
our time which is short. While I was at Bethel I saw several Yankee
skulls that were taken up by our boys as for myself I dont want any of
them.

Jace Conley and Mat Fullwood are getting well of fever. Would
you like to see us all at home again? If you will look out you will see us

in three weeks. I hear that we will leave here for home the 6th of Nov. I wish it was tomorrow. I have written this in a hurry and if you cant read it lay it away until I get home and I will read it for you. Give my best respects to sister Puss and tell her to have her new dress finished.

Good bye Dearest.

Lewis

Note: Since the above was written I learn that Gen. Magruder says that we have to start to Bethel at 3 P. M. and that there will be only one tent sent from each company. I will not go down today as I am suffering with a cold.

L

Pleasant Hill, NC
October 26th 1861

My dear dear Friend,

This evening I have concluded to drop you a few lines although I feel like anything else but writing; I am suffering with the headache and also with the blues   I have been expecting a letter from you for a week. I went to Morganton yesterday   thought sure I would get a letter from Yorktown, but was again disappointed   I can hear of no one that has got a letter lately   I cant imagine why some of you dont write unless you are all sick or that old tyrant McGruder will not let you have time to write. I do think you ought to write when you know we are so anxious to hear from you, if you were like some of my correspondents I would not often be disappointed in receiving a letter, I received a letter yesterday and it has taken half of today to read it — it is written on very large letter paper interlined and cross lined   I never saw as much writing on one sheet of paper, and it is one continuation of big words from beginning to the close for high flown language I pronounce it unsurpassed by modern effort. I dont see how I am to answer it for I cant comprehend   I suppose I will wait until you come home and get you to assist me. will you? there is preaching at Sardis tomorrow. I have been thinking that by the time of preaching there again you would be at home if nothing happens but when I think of the uncertainty of life and the many dangers to which you are exposed I know it is very doubtful about your getting home yet but I do hope and pray that you will have no fight or any more deaths in the company and that you may all be permitted to return home safe with "a star shining on your breasts" I have heard of the fight at Leesburg. I think the Yankees were worse panic struck there than any place yet from the way they pitched into the river; there must have been a great many drowned. I can not help feeling sorry for the poor deluded mortals when I think of so many being hurried into eternity   I fear unprepared.

It has been raining almost incessantly this evening   I fear we will have another freshet. I do sympathize with the poor soldiers these cold rainy days and nights   I wish all those diabolical politicians were ex-

posed to the severest weather perhaps it would bring them to a sense
of duty. The cavalry company meets again today in Morganton   I believe they meet once every week   they say they will leave in two or
three weeks but to give you my private opinion I dont think they will
leave before December. Sunday evening. I have just returned from
preaching   we heard a splendid sermon today. Mr. Shippe preaches
only once more for us before he goes to conference. I hope you will be
here to go with me to preaching that time   I heard today that Capt
Avery had written he did not know when you would get home   I was
greatly surprised to hear it   I cant understand what he means   If you
dont get home in Nov I think I shall give up in despair. Oh! do, do,
do come if you cant come no other way I want you all to join and
fight your way home   You must come home if you dont you will see
Sue Moore and Neal coming to Yorktown one of these days. I want
you to give old Magruder my compliments and tell him that the <u>Sugar
sticks</u> and <u>band box</u> boys will not fight under him any more after they
are disbanded. I think their object is to get you to join the state troops
I would see old Magruder in Yankeedom first   I would not be forced
into anything   I suppose I will have to quit as Puss Alexander is waiting on me to go a visiting with her to night. I will beg Puss to write
some. Tell John Suddreth Sue is well and complains that he does not
write to her   tell him I say shame on him for such conduct   I told
Sue I would not write unless he did although I write myself and get no
letters.

Yours as ever
Cornelia

NOTE: *Written across the top of the first page:*

I had almost forgotten to ask you to write   Will you be so kind as to
drop your unworthy friend a line or two in reply to this badly composed scrap   I wrote to Tom Parks last week and give him all the
news I could think of   Puss says I shall not write any more for she
wants to start   May heavens richest blessings rest upon you

goodbye

On October 21, 1861, Union troops commanded by Colonel Edward D. Baker attacked Confederate Brigadier General Nathanial G. Evans's brigade near Leesburg, Va. Colonel Baker was killed on the field and his men were driven back in such a panic that numbers of them rushed into the Potomac River and were drowned. Colonel Baker was a United States senator from Oregon and a personal friend of President Lincoln.

The other letter Cornelia received was written by Samuel Erwin Penland. This letter is in the McGimsey Papers and is still difficult to understand.

"Neal" is a reference Cornelia is making to herself.

The First Regiment N.C. Volunteers was mustered out of the Confederate Service on November 12, 1861. It returned to Raleigh on November 13 and was mustered out of state service the same day. Corporal Lewis Warlick returned home to Burke County and proposed marriage. He had kept all of the letters Cornelia had sent over the past six months and he stored them for safe keeping.

Captain C. Moulton Avery became a Lt. Colonel, 33rd Regiment, N.C. Troops.

Robert Vance Kerley (Cousin Bob) enlisted as a sergeant in Company B, 54th Regiment N.C. Troops. He later became a 2nd Lieutenant.

Calvin S. Brown became Captain of Company D of the 11th Regiment N.C. Troops. Brown offered to support Lewis Warlick as a Lieutenant in his company.

Charlie McGimsey immediately joined his brother John, Bartlett Sisk, Will Avery and other Burke County sons in Company F, 41st Regiment, N.C. Troops, which had organized in October as a cavalry regiment.

In January 1862, Union Major General Ambrose Everett Burnside began an expedition into northeastern North Carolina. His army captured Roanoke Island in February, New Bern in March, and Beaufort and Fort Macon in April. Washington, North Carolina and Plymouth, North Carolina soon fell to Federal occupation.

On March 31, 1862, some men from the old Company G completed reorganization as Company B and became part of the 11th Regiment, N.C. Troops. This was the successor to the old "Bethel Regiment" and the new regiment was entrusted with the Bethel Regiment flag. Their first assignment was to help defend eastern North Carolina. Mark D. Armfield was the first company Captain. Thomas Parks enlisted as a First Lieutenant and later became the company Captain. Tom's younger brother H. Harrison Parks enlisted as a private. Port Warlick returned and became a 2nd Lieutenant. Bill McGimsey and Phifer Erwin enlisted as Sergeants. Elam Bristol also returned as a Sergeant and brought his younger brother Lambert along as a private. A. Pinkney Warlick, a younger brother to both Lewis and Port, and Sid Wakefield enlisted together as privates.

By May, 1862 Cornelia and Lewis were still not married. The Confederacy was asking for more men, and Lewis went to Wilmington, N.C. to visit his friends and brothers. While visiting, he joined Company B of the 11th Regiment as a private and continued writing letters to Cornelia. Lewis was probably the only person from the "Old Bethel" to reenter service at a lower rank.

The letters that Lewis received from Cornelia during the last three years of the war are lost.

The State Troops and the Volunteers both had regiments with the same numbers 1–10. There was a 1st Regiment N.C. Volunteers and a 1st Regiment N.C. Troops. In order to eliminate confusion the Volunteer regiments from 1–14 were redesignated 11–24. Since this change took place after the First Regiment dissolved, the 11th was reorganized with slightly less than half of the men from the original regiment. In other organizations, the 2nd Regiment N.C. Volunteers became the 12th Regiment N.C. Troops, the 3rd Regiment N.C. Volunteers became the 13th Regiment N.C. Troops, etc. Sam Penland explained his feelings about the numerical change in the next letter.

Fort Lee, Virginia
Nov 30th 1861

My Dear Cousin Corrie

There are times when all is bright, but it was never intended that such happiness should continue here unallayed, else we should forget from whence it came. I was much pleased with your pleasant and exceedingly interesting letter of the 14th. I am sure I didn't think then that the "world was cold and heartless". — the same evening I rec'd one from my brother in the 29th Regt. That was calculated to change my feelings — They passed through Petersburg this week on their way to East Tennessee. I have no doubt they will see hard times this winter. Brother is a Lieut. In Capt. Robeson's company which has been very unfortunate, two of their men died at Raleigh, and many more were sick. Dr. Vale, a citizen has just returned from Lynchburg and Richmond, he saw the 29th. Talked with the Col. (R. B. Vance) (a brother of our former Capt. and now Col. of the 26th.) says the enemy have been driven back 30 miles from the Cumberland Gap, and they will probably go on to Kentucky. A battle is daily expected at Manassas. We may have the pleasure of participating. Our Col. (Junius Daniel) has been to Richmond — came down this evening. Whenever he goes he will be willing to go, whether as the 4th or the 14th.

The authorities have seen propper to change the 4th to the 14th. By numbering the 10 Regts. of regulars first. Of course we are partial to the 4th and will claim it — let things work as they will some of Carolinas sons will be in every battle. I am glad I am a carolinian, and with pride refer to "Buncombe" as my home — The state has 30,000 in the field—over 1200 of them from the good old union county of "Buncombe"—long did her brave sons strive for the union of "other and better days" and almost served the "<u>Stars</u> and <u>Strips</u>" but when <u>they</u> were <u>disgraced</u> and became the <u>colors</u> of the oppressors, the Buncombe boys rallied to the "Flag of the free". The Patriots Flag, the Flag that has and will flutter to the breeze over many a hard fought field—the glorious "Stars and bars"—The synonim of Liberty in the dark dreary future, when the last requiem of the once, honored "Stars and Stripes" shall have been sung. I read the Presidents message today; how can the deluded people of the North peruse it with hard feelings of remorse? Can men who are alike dead to shame and honor feel remorse? Can they who commit such depredations,—they whose, morals are masked by deeds of crime and darkness feel the pangs of an injured conscience? never! never! Their final reward awaits them.—"The wages of sin is death."

Cousin please excuse digression and I will return to your letter the letter of letters— Your request was a very modest one, you asked but little;—were I to "write all I could think of" and then abridge or condense it, there is no telling how small space it would occupy. Didn't you expect to offend me when you said you were willing to deny yourself the pleasure of long letters, that I might employ my time more agreeably! What other conclusion can I give to that, than you either think there are others / or something to whom, I would rather devote my leisure moments; or that I cannot appreciate your intellectual productions? One or both may be true, but I must confess I do not feel either is very complementary. however, as you were not well I will attribute that to ill health, and indulge the hope that you are quite well. I expected you to acknowledge the reception of friendship's gift and owe you an apology for not acknowledging yours, and my indebtedness for such a memento. I do not doubt but you spoke the sentiments of your heart,—consistincy and propriety may forbid the expression of mine. The letter referred to did not disturb my "pleasant hours". You apprehend no danger of those compliments having a serious effect upon me, I am not too sure, but your ... What a happy invention cousins are!—without tramping the corns of the elite,—infringing upon the "Etiquette of the day" and without the least impropriety, I can address you as my own loved cousin Corrie.

Nothing could give me more pleasure than to accept your kind invitation. I know I would enjoy a visit to Burke. I like the solitude of country life, much better than noise of the city. I have tried both. Let those who prefer the confusion and commotion of the latter, enjoy it. but give to me rural home far away from its sin and lust, where with the loved I may enjoy the sweet seclusion of a happy home. There let me live, there may I, some beautiful autumn morn when the sky is clear, bid adieu to things terrestrial, and the soul swings its way to the celestial climes of immortals land, where contention, strife "wars and rumors of wars" never come.

I am very sorry I can't come at Christmas, but must forego the pleasure a few months long; sometime next May, when nature shall have doned her prettiest garb, I think I will come. I couldn't get a furlough for more than 10 or 12 days, it would take most of that time to go and come; and I would not go that near home without going there.

Three Yankee steamers anchored on the river near Smithfield today; there is nothing to prevent them from landing and taking possession of the town at any hour. "Look out! Breakers ahead."

Please excuse all errors and write soon to

Your Affectionate Cousin

Erwin

Samuel Erwin Penland was promoted to sergeant in 1862, then reduced in rank after being absent without leave. Sam Penland was taken prisoner at Gettysburg and exchanged in 1864. After the war he settled in Clay County, N.C.

Chapter 2

Eastern North Carolina and Southside Virginia

Camp Davis near Wilmington
May 21st 1862

Dearest Cornelia,

Perhaps you would like to know what has become of me and thinking you would I have concluded to pen you a few lines before the sun begins to poring his rays from the Maredian. You will see by the heading of this that I have got down in the turpentine country and sand where the staple production is peanuts and tallow-faced women. I told you I intended going home this week, but since I came here I have come to the conclusion to remain from the fact if I was to go home the conscript act would soon bring me into service and upon the whole I think it is but time for me stay where I am acquainted and furthermore I feel better now than I have in three months—haven't had a chill or been sick since I arrived in camps, getting stronger every day.

I have not joined any company yet nor dont know which I will Brown's or Armfields. Brown has a vacancy of Lieutenant in his company and desires me to join, says he will use his influence for my election but I'm almost afraid to join him for fear I would be defeated and then have to remain in the ranks which I would not like in that company, I'd prefer being a private in Armfields. I wish you were here to advise me, but that wouldn't do for I adhered to your council last winter when I could have got a position and now am about to go in the service for the war as high private. This war cruel war I wish it was at an end and we could see our country once more enjoying the peace we once had but alas I fear many weeks and months will pass away before such is the case. If it was not for my darling sweetheart at home these troublesome times would pass more swiftly but my mind is always upon her and the time drags heavily.

Your sincere Lover
Lewis

Margin Note: Give my kindest regards to Susan & Puss and say to them if they have beaux in the army to write often to them for it makes a fellow feel mighty well for him to get a letter from his "gal". Lieut. Parks passed just now and told me to give you his best respects and would write you soon. Write often and I will try and do the same.

James Charles Sheffield McDowell, 2nd Lieutenant in the "old Bethel" Regiment, recruited Company B of the 54th Regiment and became the first Captain. Bob Kerley, Byron Kibler, and Tom Galloway were some of the men from the "old Bethel" who joined him. McDowell offered Lewis a position, but Cornelia persuaded him not to accept. McDowell later advanced to Colonel of the Regiment. He was mortally wounded during the Chancelorsville campaign, and died May 8, 1863.

Camp Davis near Wilmington
June 3rd 1862

Dearest Cornelia

Yours of the 25th Inst. came to hand yesterday which was gladly received and now am about to respond but feel incapable of doing so.

You say this is the first time in life you ever experienced a sad disappointment and was done by one who you thought would give you the least trouble, that I came off without telling you good bye or even tell you I was not going back; now you seem to think that it was intentional on my part that I knew very well when I left you that I did not expect to go back home but to remain.

I did not for a moment suppose that you would even sinuate, much less to say I had treated you badly; did I not explain to you in my last why it was that I did stay? I think I did. You say I ought to go home and hire a substitute, that I guess would be a hard job for men are so scarce at home I would not know where to get one that would be received in my place, and further more I would not get one if I could from the fact that it shall not be thrown up to my relations in future years that you had an uncle, brother, or that your father or perhaps grandfather would not go into the service when he was called on to assist his country in this great struggle for independence—was too cowardly, afraid of the Yankees & but hired a substitute to be shot at in my stead never never shall it be said of me or any descendants; death before dishonor. Dear Corrie you very well know that it is hard for me to leave you but I consider I am doing rightly. I think my first duties are to my country and then to you. I hope I may be spared to see the end of the war and then you and I will marry and try and live a happy life in the future. I pray do not sensure me for treating you badly if I have done so it was not intended   it makes me feel badly to think that you blame me for every thing I do that is not according to your views.

I have wanted to go into the service ever since last winter but you refused to let me come. I could have come against your remonstrances but did not want to do any thing to wound your feelings, which I have never done on purpose to my knowledge, but yet you say I have. Enough of that and I will write something else.

Before this reaches you   you will have heard of the great slaughter at richmond Saturday & Sunday the particulars of which we have not got yet only telegrams   all quiet there yesterday up to noon. We had marching orders last week but have never heard the word march. It was said by the Col. that our destination would be Weldon.

Last week the blockading squadron captured the steamer Gordon off Fort Caswell from Bermuda bound for Wilmington   her cargo consisted partly in five thousand stand of arms and twenty tons powder which would have been some little help to our army; we could hear the report of the guns very distinctly while they were firing on her.

Last week three of the squadron engaged the batteries at fort Fisher   after firing over a hundred shots they withdrew, the only damage done was that of a shell killing a negro woman and chicken the chicken being carried by the negro.

I have joined Armfields company. Last week I had a severe attack of the diarrhea, am getting better I dont think I'll have any more chills. You said you wanted some paper, I have plenty such as it is but I dont know how I will send it to you, I will send the first opportunity, in this I'll send some stamps. Jackson has been doing good service dont you think so! I hope he is in Baltimore this morning and then will right about march and come on Washington in the rear and burn it up and capture old Abe that would be too good.

This is so badly written I dont know whether you can read it or not. Write often to your devoted lover

Lewis

Margin Note: Give my kindest regards to Puss and all my friends.

"Slaughter at Richmond" refers to the Battle of Seven Pines May 31–June 1, 1862, a victory for no one with huge losses on both sides. Joseph E. Johnston, commanding the Confederate Army of Virginia was wounded and replaced by Robert E. Lee. Lee immediately renamed the army The Army of Northern Virginia.

Camp Wyatt near Ft. Fisher N. C.
June 17th '62

Dearest Corrie

Yours of the 9th Inst. came to hand a few days since which was gladly received and perused with much pleasure.

You asked me to send my type, that I would willingly do as the one you have is a poor specimen of the original, if I had an opportunity of getting one taken but I am twenty miles from Wilmington, the nearest place I could get one, and dont know when I will get permission to go there. I'm not free as I was at home, have to have a pass to go any where and very seldom get that. I left your picture at home locked up if I had known I was going to stay I would have brought it along, but now I dont know how I shall get it—wish you would have a good one taken and send to me. Will you? As for rain we have some occasionally not so much as you have had in Burke. We left camp Davis on last Friday, marched fifteen miles and bivouacked for the night at a beautiful spring and the next day we came on here with the intention of going into the barracks that the 2nd regiment had left, but when we arrived we found that the whole place was covered with fleas and our Colonel said we should not take quarters there at all, but marched us to a grove and ordered our tents immediately from camp Davis which we got the next evening. I have done a god deal of marching since this war broke out but of all the heavy marches I ever tried this country beats them all. The sand that is loose sand is six inches deep and you can imagine how difficult it would be to walk in that.

We are stationed between the Atlantic and Cape Fear river three quarters of a mile from the former and a quarter from the latter. I was over on the beach a day or two ago and could plainly see six blockading steamers, not more than five miles distant   after looking at them awhile I walked down the beach to Fort Fisher, and by the way it is the most beautiful beach I ever saw, the sand where the tide has receded is as hard almost as a floor which makes it first rate walking. After viewing the fort I started back to camps and was hailed by the sentinel but after telling some stories we were allowed to pass   we told the sentinel we were in charge of a Lieut who we pointed out and he (Waddell) said he was a commissioned officer, the sentinel remarked that he hadn't on an officers uniform   no said Waddell I dont wear it on every occasion, the sentinel then asked him for his commission. Waddell replied that he had left it at the camps, after many questions asked by the sentinel he called the corporal and sergeant they let us through the lines after repeating to them what we had told the sentinel. We would not have gone without a pass, but it was the same day we moved to this place and there had been no guard, thrown out and we were at liberty to go where we pleased. I failed to tell you the way we got into the fort, we crawled in at a post hole and after we got in there we didn't know that there would be any difficulty in getting out at the regular pass way or we would have gone back thought the way we came. We lost two members last week of fever, David Keller of Caldwell and Tolbert Harbison and I suppose by this time there is another dead a young man by the name of Morgan   he was left at Camp Davis and I heard this morning that he was dying and besides him we have one in Wilmington in the hospital, John Puett, who it is said is very ill and very doubtful of his recovery. We have bad luck with our sick and I dont attribute it to any thing only a lack of surgeons who know something about medicine. I haven't much faith in ours although they may understand the practice of medicine better than I think they do; our assistant surgeon cant be a very skillful physician as he is only about twenty one or two years of age.

I haven't had a chill since I left home and dont think I'll have any more of the Yorktown chills but may take them in the North Carolina swamps when August rolls around. It is said that this is a healthy place but I dont think it can be as the water is remarkably bad. All the boys from our section are in good health I believe but Bob Carlton   he is complaining of a severe cold. You wanted to know if I thought we would have any fight down here soon, well I dont think we will unless we are whipped at Richmond and then I think it would be quite likely we would have a brush with the rascals. We have good news in camps but dont know the certainty of it is this; there are seventeen English men-of-war lying in Hampton Roads and Lord Lyons has demanded his passport and has returned to England and furthermore that France has acknowledged the independence of the Confederate States; all of which is very good if true but will not vouch for the certainty of it. I will close for I know you will get tired of reading so much. Give my kindest regards to sister Puss. Write often to your devoted

Lover

Lewis

Margin Note: I hope now soon the war may end and then I know there will be some happiness for me if I should be so fortunate as to see that end.

⸻ ❖ ⸻

John Morgan died at Camp Davis on June 18, 1862.

Camp Wyatt was named for Private Henry Lawson Wyatt of Company A, 1st Regiment, N.C. Infantry, who had died the previous summer while fighting with Lewis at Bethel Church, Virginia. As previously mentioned, Wyatt was the first Confederate soldier to die in battle in the Civil War.

Duncan C. Waddell was a private in Company G, Eleventh Regiment, from Chatham County, N.C. He was appointed First Lt. in July, 1863 "for gallant conduct on the field at Gettysburg."

Wilmington, N. C.
June 24th 1862

My Dearest Friend,

Again I am about to drop you a few lines, but you need not expect to gain much information from them as I have only a small store of news on hand but knowing that you would like to get a sheet and envelope at any time from me even if there was only the words I am well, and my signature; therefore I concluded I would give the mail a small burden consisting of the foregoing articles if no more.

You will see by the head of this that we have changed camp again; on the 18th Inst. We got marching orders (being there at camp Wyatt) for Petersburg Va. we at once went to work and prepared two days rations and was put on the march that evening for this place and arrived the next morning very much fatigued from the heavy march through the heavy sand, I fell out on the way from a pain in my left hip, rested awhile and started overtaking the regiment at the next resting place, and from that on I kept along with the rear guard although suffering a good deal from the pain. After arriving here the order was countermanded, then officers as well as privates began to grumble, as they did not wish to return to camp Wyatt on account of the heavy roads and the great hatred they had for the former camp; they all expressed a desire to go on to Richmond or join Jackson rather than go back among those fleas that are so numerous. I will relate what one of Col. Tews' men told me and then you can imagine how plentiful they were (by the way we took the place of Col. Tews' regiment (2nd) at Camp Wyatt he having been ordered to report in Richmond, he said you might take up a bucket of sand at night and by the next morning it would be all jumped out. What do you think of that? How would you like to live where there are so many of the troublesome little fellows? I forgot to say that after the order was countermanded we got orders to remain here until further orders, which was received with smiling countenances. It is not known how long we will stay here or where we will go to when we leave, my opinion is that we will be ordered to Va. before long; there has been two regiments gone on since we came up here one being a Geo(rgia). And

the other the 43rd N.C. that came up from Smithville after us, des-
tined for Va.

Gen. Beaureaguard and staff passed through two nights since and
a week or two previous Gen. Price and staff also all bound for Richmond, and by the papers I learn that a portion of their army is now on
their way. It seems that Richmond is to be held at all hazards; there
will be one of the most bloody battles before long you ever heard of in
modern times, I think the whipping we are going to give them there
will be the means of effecting a peace. R. V. Michaux and Asbury
Puett arrived night before last. Mr. Puett's son is very ill, don't get any
better cant hold out much longer unless a change. You speak of visiting us here if we remain this summer – wish you would come now –
would like to see you even if you would look sour at me for not telling
you good bye, never mind the next time I leave you I will tell you
good bye twice. I wish the war was over and I was on Linville; don't
you?

You must go down to "dads" house some of these times and see
Harriet. I wish I could be at home next Sunday I would get to see you
at Mountain Grove. I know you will be there with your flowered dress
or a new one. There is the place to buy cheap goods when you come
down you can by in a supply; calico is worth only $1.00 per yard and
every thing else in proportions.

Your goodest friend
Lewis

----

*General Pierre Gustave Toutant Beauregard commanded Confederate troops
at Charleston and arranged the surrender of Ft. Sumter. He then commanded
troops at First Manassas. After quarreling with President Davis, he was sent
to the west. He spent the rest of 1861 and the spring of 1862 in Mississippi,
Tennessee, and Kentucky. In June of 1862 he was given command of the Dept.
of South Carolina and Georgia. Beauregard was on his way to his new command when this letter was written .*

John Wesley Puett died June 25, 1862.

Wilmington, N. C.
July 5th 1862

Dearest Cornelia,

Why is it that you dont write, three weeks have lapsed since I
heard from you and I am uneasy for fear there is something the matter. I have been looking with great anxiety for the last two weeks for
letters and have received none. Perhaps you have no paper as you
wrote to me some time since that you were out. if that be the case you
are excusable otherwise I dont think you would be. I suppose you get
the news from the Richmond fight regularly   terrible fighting there
wasn't it? and I am glad to know that our forces are still pushing the
enemy back. The last dispatch I have seen from the battle field was up
to night before last. Then the enemy was in full retreat in Charles City
county and our forces in pursuit. I hope they will kill and capture the
last one of them. Already we have killed and captured thousands including five Generals captured one being next in command to Mc-
Clellan (Maj Gen McCall)   Many wounded and dead are passing
through every day; yesterday the remains of Col. Mears, of the 3rd
Reg. was brought in — was killed at Richmond his body will be in-
terred at the Cemetery to day with military honors our regiment being
ordered out as an escort.

If we had gone on to Va. When we were ordered we would have
been participants in that great battle; and then perhaps some of us
would have breathed our last, notwithstanding all these considerations
I would like to have been there to help drive back these heartless in-
vaders from our beloved soil.

Our company left here last night at 10 for Masonboro sound
eight miles distant to unload a schooner that run the blockade and is
now in port safe. The reason I did not go was that it looked very much
like raining and I have a cold and was fearful if I got wet it would
make me sick, and besides that I had a pain in my right eye, therefore
I concluded it would be better for me to remain in camps. Two companies of our regiment have been for the last week unloading a valuable cargo near Fort Fisher; the vessel was the Modern Greece from
England, in attempting to run in the port the blockaders cut her off

and also got in her rear then the only chance for her to keep from falling as a prize into the hands of the Yankees was to beach her which was done in three fourths of a mile of Fort Fisher. The steamer is a total wreck and only about two thirds of the cargo (900 tons) was saved; her cargo consisted of seven thousand stand of arms, twenty seven hundred and seventy barrels of powder, gray cloth, domestic clothing, medicine, shoes, wines, brandies, salt, pepper, spice, cannon in fact every thing you could think of. There is now another steamer lying outside the blockaders watching for an opportunity to run in. What kind of a time did you have at the quarterly meeting? Did you get the paper I sent you? I will send you more before long, if I can some better than that was. I think I will go down to the sound this evening and help the boys get off that cargo if it clears off. Write often and a great deal to your kindest friend and _____

Lewis

Margin Note:

give my best respects to sister and Susan. Lt. Parks had an other chill yesterday; Port, Pink and H. Parks are well. Wm. McGimsey has been unwell but is getting better.

⸺•⋯•⸺

The Seven Days Campaign lasted from June 25 to July 1, 1862. This was General Robert E. Lee's first field command of the Army of Northern Virginia. All of the fighting was around Richmond, and by the end of the campaign McClellan's threat to Richmond was in retreat.

Camp Lamb, Wilmington
July 21st 1862

Dearest Corrie,

I received a short note from you a few days since of eight pages and you promised the next time you wrote you would write a long letter; which I am looking for every day. Those "short notes" you write please me very well, I wish you would often get in the spirit of writing such ones.

I'm sorry to say I cant write such "notes" as I have nothing to write and furthermore I cannot compose a letter that ought to be shown to or criticized upon by anyone but the author. We still have a good deal of sickness in camp. several cases of fever in the regiment. Last week we lost another man, Pomp Justis of fever who is the eighth to have left us by death. I was sorry to hear a few days since of the death of Cousin Port Warlick who was wounded in the head below Richmond taken home and died of Neuralgia; he was a fine young man and bid fair to become a bright ornament to society, his brother Pink also a Lt. was wounded at Seven Pines but has almost recovered of his wounds. I had a good many relatives from Catawba and Lincoln killed and wounded at Richmond. I understand Gen. French has been ordered to Petersburg to take command of Eastern North Carolina and portion of Eastern Va in place of Gen. Holmes, he having been ordered to another field. Col Leventhorpe now takes command of this district, so report says. I cant vouch for the certainty as it is hard to get at the truth of anything now-a-days. I went out in the country yesterday and got as many peaches and watermelons as I wanted by paying a big price. Everything is very dear in Wilmington, peaches worth forty cents per doz   watermelons, large $2.00, potatoes $1.00 bus   tomatoes 20cts qt   onions 10cts do   and everything in proportion to that I have named and the worst of it is we have no money. I haven't drawn a cent since I've been in the service, and dont know when I will; but if I had money I would spend it and get but little for it   so upon the whole it is best I haven't any. If you will gather a load of peaches an bring them down you can make almost a fortune out of them at the present prices. I'll buy four dozen anyway   provided you trust me, if not, cant purchase.

I cant say wether Port and Hattie are in earnest or not he never tells me anything about it. I know they still keep up a correspondence. Our band train and instruments have arrived after so long a time. I hope we will have some music now to cheer us up when we get depressed in spirit.

Col. Leventhorpe has succeeded in getting a chaplain for the regiment. Rev. Mr. Smith an Episcopal minister I think   a minister of some other denomination would have been more acceptable than he, as there are but few of that "stripe" in our midst; the Col. has got his choice and I reckon we ought to be satisfied; he is a member of that "aristocratic church" and seems to be a very good man. One thing I do know is that there is but few better officers of his rank in the state.

At any time that you can send me a cheese and a pair of socks they will be very acceptable. I must tell you what we are going to have for desert today, a nice peach pie. I board with the non coms and a splendid cook we have too. Ed a servant of Jones Erwin. I can say when we have money to buy we live well and are willing to go their proportional part in anything which makes quite an agreeable mess.

We have had for the last two or three weeks as warm weather as ever I saw in any country, at any rate it seemed to me so.

All the boys from our part of the country are well except Sid Wakefield, who is a little unwell, though getting better. My health is tolerably good, able to do all the duty assigned me but not willing as you very well know I never had a great thirst for any kind of labor. Say to Puss I approve of her economy these hard times and recommend that you follow her example. Give her my kindest regards. As ever your affectionate

Lewis

Collett Leventhorpe was born in England and attained the rank of captain in the British Army before emigrating to Rutherford County, N.C. He was appointed colonel of the 34th Regiment and transferred to the 11th Regiment in 1862. He was wounded in the left arm at Gettysburg, then captured and held in several Federal hospitals and prisons before being exchanged in March 1864. Leventhorpe resigned in April, 1864, because of his wounds.

Cousins Port and Pink Warlick were not just cousins, but double first cousins. It seems that Lewis' cousins had the same names as his brothers, but in carrying this one step further, these cousins had another brother named Lewis.

Brigadier General Samual Gibbs French was a West Point graduate from New Jersey who sided with the South.

Ed, the servant of Jones Erwin, was in camp with George Phifer Erwin, Mr. Erwin's son. Phifer mentioned Ed in most of his letters home.

Hattie Jewell maintained a correspondence with Lewis' brother Portland.

Camp Lamb, Wilmington N.C.
Aug. 17th 1862

Dearest Corrie,

You will please pardon me for not writing sooner the only objection I have to render is that the extreme hot weather prevented me from the hard task. It has been so extremely hot for the last fortnight that it made me so uncommonly lazy that I could scarcely do anything in doors or out; never have I experienced such scorching weather in the old North State, it seemed to me that I would suffocate any how; the suns reflections from the sand, I think was the cause of such great heat as then in an abundance of that in this low country; now the weather is quite pleasant there being a change yesterday.

You stated in your last letter that you were going to town to have your teeth worked on that I said you must have it done, well that, I have no doubt is so as you said, "you must etc." but I was thinking I said you ought, that dont matter. I'm glad you got them fixed for I dont want you to have a full mouth of gums and no teeth when we get married, for then someone might laugh at you as I know you laugh about a certain young lady putting her hand to her mouth when she laughed to keep others from seeing her old "snags". I have had two of mine filled since I came to Wilmington and the dentist only charged me eight ($8.00) dollars, high enough dont you think? I also have three others that need filling but I will wait till I can get some one to do it cheaper if there are any such.

I suppose ere this you have heard of the arrival of the Steamer "Kate" from Nassau to this port with a valuable cargo of arms, ammunition etc. I was orderly for the General Court Martial and was in the third story of the Post Office, which is near the warf, looked out of the window and saw her coming most beautifully up the river, went down stairs immediately and proceeded to the warf and went on board to hear the news and to have it said that I was on board of a vessel that had been so fortunate as to get in by the blockading squadron without a single shot being fired; the previous day to her arrival she was chased by a Yankee cruiser six hours, but the swiftness of the Kate left her on the briny deep without a prize. The Kate is now on the dry dock receiving repairs and being cleaned preparatory to taking another voyage, she will carry out a cargo of cotton. The Kate is a beautiful steamer of light draft owned in the Confederate States but carries English colors; this being the ninth time she has succeeded in running the blockade, lucky isn't she. Since I last wrote you we got marching orders again to go to Kinston but before we got ready for the trip, they were countermanded.

Sid Wakefield is chilling occasionally also H. Galloway and E. B. Bristol. I must tell you what was done by the members of company B; there was a petition written out and signed by sixty out of seventy two; that was all that was present for Lt. E. W. Dorsey to resign his position as third Lt. and sent on to Morganton, since we have not heard from it. In the petition was written why it was that we asked him to resign, which was that he was not qualified to fill the position that he holds and that it would be doing the service a great good for him to do so etc. If he does resign I think there will be a chance for me to get a little higher, at least I'll be a candidate, but dont tell any body, for fear he wont resign and some one may say that I signed the petition on purpose to get into office. As ever your

Lewis

———◆·•·◆———

Elisha Wesley Dorsey did not resign. He was wounded and captured at Gettysburg. He had his right leg amputated while in federal hospitals, and was exchanged in December, 1864. He was promoted to First Lieutenant while a prisoner of war.

Lewis was obviously ambitious. On August 19, 1862, he was promoted to Corporal.

Topsail Sound, N. C.
Aug. 29th 1862

My Dearest Friend,

Yours of the 20th Inst. came to hand last night which was gladly received.

You said that you hadn't received any letters from me for some time. I dont know why it was that you did not for I wrote nearly every week I was at Wilmington. You stated that if I was sick or couldn't pay postage that I was excusable, but laziness was no excuse. Well in the first place I am happy and thankful to the all wise being that I can inform you that I have had good health, and as to postage, I have been fortunate enough after so long a time to have plenty of money. I first drew my Confederate and then State, County and more than that I sold my watch for seventy ($70.00) dollars so you see I have plenty of money to defray all expenses.

I'm sorry to hear that John and Sue have made a final separation, 'tis hard after courting for six years and then burst up without having the ties of connubial bliss entwined around their pathway for life; I hope nothing will ever bring us to experience the same fate as that of our friends. And Sue has another beau   well she is very fortunate as to get another so soon these war times when all the flowers of the country is in the service. I cant imagine who he is. Please tell me.

You had those teeth extracted   well I suppose you look old now. Did you have any of your fore teeth taken out? I will send you stamps, paper and my type when I get back to Wilmington.

John McGimsey came to out camp last night; he is not looking well. We came to this place a week since, only two companies   A and B   the other part of the regiment is at camp Davis. I suppose we were sent here to picket as we send pickets out every night near the new Topsail Inlet which is two miles from camp. This inlet is deep enough for any of the enemy's gunboats to run in and get in the sound where they could lie if they chose. On the day we arrived here there was a schooner run in with eight hundred sacks of salt without any hindrance as the Inlet is not blockaded. All along the sound there are salt works making a great quantity of salt and selling at a high price; at our camp are three works now in operation and another in course of construction, now being very extensive.

I'm glad we were ordered away from Wilmington as it was very unhealthy there; here I think we will have better health as our sick are now improving without a physician, both being with the regiment.

My health is better now than it has been since Christmas for which I am very thankful. We get oysters, fish, clams, roasting ears, etc. tolerable plenty. This is a very good country down here, land is very productive and is very level. Dorsey hasn't come yet and I dont care if he never does for he is no more use to the company than the fifth wheel to a wagon. I wish he would resign and give some man his position that deserves it for I very well know he does not.

I dont know when I will get a furlough to go home, I would like very much to go at any time but it is almost impossible for any well man to get one. Write often to your devoted friend and lover

Lewis

Margin Note: Give Puss my kindest regards and tell her I could not comply with her request to help her cut that peach pie, nothing prevented but the distance that intervenes.

Say to Miss Susan that I said "   ...   " she is very unfortunate to court a man six years and then kick him, tell her if she will not promise to do me likewise I will be her beau very soon for I see very clearly that you and I will never jump the broom. Dont forget to write. Direct as before. We are twenty one miles from Wilmington but there will be the best place to get our letters.

John W. McGimsey was Cornelia's nephew in Company F, 41st Regiment, N.C. Troops. He was a brother of Bill, Charlie, and Theodore McGimsey, who have been mentioned in other letters.

Camp Davis N. C.
Sept. 16th 1862

Dearest Corrie,

Yours of the 3rd Inst. came to hand yesterday long time getting here. You complain that you get no letters from me. I dont know why it is I wrote to you twice while at Topsail and got but one from you so you see I write oftener than you. The four companies that were at Topsail got marching orders last Saturday evening for Wilmington and after making ready one days rations; started about 8 at night marched all night and reached Wilmington on Sunday morning where they were joined by the other six companies from this place; did not remain there long till it got orders to march here at once as the Yellow Fever was raging in Wilmington, the six companies came on immediately but the other four were so much fatigued from their march the night previous, they only came out three miles and halted until the next morning. I escaped the hard march on Saturday night by being detailed to take care of the baggage. I didn't leave Topsail till Sunday morning and then I got to drive part of the way which was very acceptable; at dark we got with the boys in three miles of Wilmington where we all bivouacked for the night — the next morning we came here.

I was in hopes when we left Topsail we were then on our way to old "Stonewall" in Maryland but alas the Yellow Fever or something else stopped us. I dislike for the Yellow Fever to be in Wilmington; on yesterday morning there were fifty new cases reported and five deaths the night previous   it has been there six weeks and the doctors did not ascertain that it was the Yellow Fever until a few days since. It was brought in by the Steamer Kate, one case it was taken to the hospital and there it began to spread till it has gotten extensively circulated in the town; all business is closed and everything doing to prevent it from getting any wider hold in the streets   they are burning turpentine and rosin — the trains not allowed to come into the depot, they stop outside not far distant. I fear we will get it into the regiment as there was a good many of the boys out in town Saturday night. It is said to be very contagious and fatal. I wish we could get to go to Maryland. I believe the whole regiment would like to do so as we are doing nothing here and I dont see that we ever will.

I have some very nice shells I wish you had but have no way of sending them. I dont like to hear of so many marrying and I have to live single so long I'm fearful I can't get a furlough to go home and get married, but then it might be I couldn't get anybody—would tell me to wait three or four months or wait and see if the war wouldn't close by the next year. I must quit writing as my breakfast is nearly ready.

Give Puss my kindest regards. I hope I'll not get to lazy to write any more. Direct as before. This is written in a hurry and if you cant read it bring it down and I will read it for you.

As ever your devoted friend and lover

Lewis

Camp Davis, N. C.
Sept. 20th 1862

My Dearest Friend,

I wrote to you only a few days since, but as I wrote the yellow Fever was raging in Wilmington and it was quite probable that our regiment would have it from imprudence; I now write to lesson any fears that you may have of the fatal disease. When I wrote to you before I stated that on the day previous there were fifty new cases reported; since I understand that that was an exaggeration, although brought from town by Capt. Bird it was not true, only in part.

There has been several cases but not half as many as we first heard.

Col. Leventhorpe came from town a few days since, he says when he left there was several cases but that it had not taken an epidemic character as yet.

I hope this may relieve you of any fears you may entertain of the malignant disease.

We lost another Captain a few days since, Capt. Jennings Co. G from Chapel Hill, he had Typhoid Fever and was sent to the hospital from thence he started home but ere he reached the station where he was to stop he died. He will be a great loss to the company and also to the regiment he being one of the best Captains in it.

Nearly every day brings us good news from our armies, the latest is that Gen. Jackson has taken Harpers Ferry with the whole company (10,000) and all the government stores; and Gen. D. H. Hill whiped McClellan in Maryland after two days hard fighting; and Gen. Price gained a victory over the Federals at Iuka capturing the place; and various other places where our arms have been victorious, of less importance.

Surely so many reverses to the enemy ought to bring them to their senses and show them that the south will never be subdued.

When I hear of our brother soldiers doing so much in Va and Maryland it makes me want to be with them for we are doing nothing here and I dont believe we ever will.

I hope you will have no cause in the future to complain of my not writing for I intend at least that is my notion now that I will write to you weekly and I want you not to forget to answer them either. We are having very warm weather for the season.

Gen. Clingman has been removed from this district and Gen. Rains takes command.

You ought to come down some evening to dress parade and see us go through the manual and hear the fine notes of the Bethel band; they are beginning to play splendidly. Dorsey was very mad when he came back and took several of the boys through a talk for us taking he said the advantage of him in his absence, he said that we the leading ones influenced a great many of the illiterate to sign it through misrepresentations, which I and others pronounced a falsehood. I told him that the thing was not misrepresented to any one but all new full well the meaning and signed it of their own free will. He says he will not resign; he knows he never will get another as for — office, but few in the company like him. Give Puss a brothers love for me. Write soon and often to

Lewis
the soldier

The Yellow Fever lasted until the first frost in November, 1862 stopped the epidemic. The fever killed an estimated 650 people and caused many residents to evacuate the city.

While Daniel Harvey Hill did have some success holding McClellan at Turner's Gap on September 15th, the main battle in Maryland at Sharpsburg on September 17th was not a good day for either the North or the South. 23,000 men were casualties on September 17, 1862, and at the end of the fighting both armies held much the same ground they had held at the beginning of the battle. Both McClellan and Lincoln claimed a victory, but McClellan was fired after the November elections.

Major General Sterling Price defeated federal forces in Iuka, Mississippi on September 17, 1862.

Frances W. Bird was Captain of Company C, in the 11th Regiment, N.C. Troops. He later played a courageous role for the entire regiment at Gettysburg.

Gabriel James Rains, of New Bern, graduated from West Point and fought in the Seminole War and the Mexican War before joining the Confederate Army as a brigadier general. His area of expertise was explosives, and he mined the waters and roadways around Yorktown. This was the first use of land mines in warfare and brought outraged protest from the North as well as the South. The practice was considered so ungentlemanly that General James Longstreet forbade their use against the enemy. Later, Confederate Secretary of War George Randolph allowed the use of land mines in limited circumstances.

General Thomas L. Clingman was a U.S. representative in the 1840s and 1850s, and served as U.S. senator from 1858 until North Carolina seceded from the union.

In October 1862, the 11th Regiment was ordered to Franklin, Virginia for defensive operations in the Blackwater River area.

Franklin, Va.
October 12th 1862

My dearest Friend

I have neglected writing to you since I came to this place in fact we have had so much to do that I havent had but little time to write to any one since arrived here on the 8th Inst. and since that time it has rained nearly all the time   have pitched our tents in three different encampments, been out on picket all night, and one day on a scout. as you can imagine that there has been but little time to write to ones sweetheart; after taking these things into consideration I have no doubt you will freely forgive for my silence.

On the day before we came here the Yankees shelled the town and woods for a half day from their gunboats and artillery beyond the river but with little injury to us, two or three wounded   it is said they lost a considerable number both on their gunboats and on land.

This place is on the Seaboard & Roanoke Rail Road 21 miles from Suffolk where the road crosses the Black Water river   it is entirely deserted by all the citizens. The river here is narrow but very deep, enough so as to float any of the enemys vessels and no obstructions until they get right up to the town. There are two boats sunk there to prevent them from assending any higher … now, a part of our Reg. is down on the river 5 miles below trying to blockade down there, don't know wether they will make an efficient one or it or not.

We have had two "long rolls" since we came but not a Yankee have I seen yet. The first time we were ordered out there was a party of them yet in a mile of the town but a few shots from our artillery soon sent them skedaddle. Yesterday the cavalry went out on a scout they met up with a company of Pennsylvania cavalry, had a little brush put the enemy to flight and brought in tow Yanks both wounded and killed two horses, none hurt on our side. I forgot to say the enemy fled when our party was the pursuers for several miles, couldnt overtake them.

We are not living so well here as we did at camp Davis. The only bread we get is cracklins which I don't like as I got tired of them on board of ship and wouldn't care if I never see another. Id rather have cornbread all the time. There is some talk of us being sent to Petersburg   wish we would although we will have 60 miles to march rather do it than stay here.

It was quiet cold last night. I fear we will suffer this winter from cold as we cannot be provided for as we should be   havent got any overcoat and a good many of us are nearly barefooted and some entirely. I have only 1 pair of socks and am saving them til I get a pair of shoes. If you have a chance send me a pr of socks. As ever your devoted friend

L

Margin notes:

We left two men at camp Davis, Pink Teem and Tom Shufler, the former very sick and the other to wait on him.

We havent any men here very sick, some having chills. I do hope I will escape them this fall. I under stand there is a large force at Suffolk and the report was afoot the other day that Gen. Longstreet with his Division was coming here to attack Suffolk.

Gen. French was down here some time since with three brigades to attack Suffolk, but from some cause or other he did not make the attempt—Marched back to Petersburg.

Our regiment is the only infantry that is here—one reg. of cavalry and one company of artillery. The 52nd was here but left for Petersburg a few days before we arrived. Direct to this place and quickly.

General Longstreet's next major campaign was at Fredericksburg; however, on April 11th in the following spring (1863) Longstreet did begin a siege at Suffolk. The siege was broken off on May 3rd when General Lee decided to move Longstreet closer to the Chancelorsville activity.

In late October Lewis received a furlough to go home. He returned to Franklin in mid-November. Many of his friends asked him to bring back shoes and other items on his return.

J. Pinkney Teem survived his illness. He was later captured at Gettysburg, exchanged in 1865 and hospitalized in Richmond near the end of the war.

Camp Nelson near Franklin Depot, VA
Nov. 19th 1862

My Dearest Friend

For the first time since my arrival I have undertaken to drop you a few lines   I would have written yesterday or day before but was prevented by what I will relate afterwards in this. I arrived on last Thursday night tired and worn out as I had in charge twenty one boxes, and I can say that it will be the last lot of boxes of that number that I ever will undertake to bring through because it is so much trouble. I was lucky to get through as soon as I did and would not have gotten here when I did if I had have had no help. I found the boys generally well in camps but since I left there has been several men sent to Petersburg to the hospital   some very ill   among the members is John Duval — has Typhoid fever.

Yesterday we had quite a lively time but I will pen what occurred the day previous. On Monday morning at 8 we were called up by the loud taps of the drum and ordered to get breakfast and be in readiness by 4 ½, at that time we were in line and at once marched to headquarters in town, Capt. Armfield, being in charge we halted, in a few minutes Col. Leventhorpe's loud voice was heard distantly all along the lines — we took up our march across Blackwater accompanied by three pieces of artillery and Col. Ferrebee's cavalry with a train of twenty three wagons the object was to go over in Isle of Wight County after forage — we marched on in the direction of Suffolk five miles when we were halted — batteries put in position and every company assigned his — The wagon to therein loading of corn, fodder & etc; here we remained til all the wagons or nearly so were loaded, all quietly. I was standing near Col. Ferrebee and others listening at their chat when I cast my eyes down the road and saw a courier coming at full speed. I will here state that there was two or three companies from the cavalry a mile and a half in advance at Carrsville, when the boy rode up he called out to Ferrebee to "bring your companies on they are fighting." I at once run for my rifle before the command "fall in" was given but before I got far all the officers were ordering "fall in" which was done quickly and off we went at double quick right after the artillery; our gait was not slacked the whole distance but that did not seem to tire me as I thought there was some prospect of a fight but not so   the cavalry drove them off before we arrived so we had a chase all for nothing; there was two persons taken—about all that was done; if there was any killed or wounded we did not find it out, after staying there awhile we commenced retracing our steps—reached our camps a little before night somewhat fatigued.

But yesterday was the time; before day the long roll called us again into line—marched to headquarters there the Col. assigned to each Captain his place—two companies beyond the river to act as skirmishers, A & G, the remaining ones on this side. The report was the enemy was advancing in large force. Pretty soon after we got our position we heard heavy firing of artillery up the river 6 or 7 miles off while that firing was going on our scouts brought in nine prisoners and reported the enemy to be in heavy force two miles off; the Col. told us that from all he could gather from the scouts and prisoners that they had a very heavy force the lowest estimate he could get was four brigades but he thought it was quite probable that was two small, but said he "I am determined to hold the place at all hazards and he hoped the Bethel regiment would still retain the reputation she had for valor" further said our force was small but he was calling for help with all his might & after he got through three hasty cheers were given for our commander. We remained in our positions til 12 or perhaps a little after then the Yanks commenced shelling our scouts rapidly which was a shade too hot for them and they came in with five men wounded   three very slightly the other two severely all from company A as soon as they and the pickets were driven in our batteries opened fire, but then the enemy had been shelling us for nearly an hour, our pickets and skirmishers prevented us from firing. When each side opened I tell you there was a thundering for two hours almost equal to the Bethel fight—bang; crash, sing went the shells and pieces all around us; you ought to have been there to have seen me dodge some time I would fall flat on the ground and then I would lie for some time and I would rise—here would come the shell down I would go again. We were all ordered to lie down but occasionally I would get up to look about but in that position I did not remain long as the shell made to much of a ratling for a man in a standing position   when he could not defend himself there we had to lie and take it all and couldn't get a shot. There was no infantry firing at all. After two hours their batteries were silenced and they skedaddled for Suffolk which relieved me of a good deal of dread. Our cavalry followed them over some distance and along the road they learned from citizens, Gen. Peck was in command with two brigades and eight pieces of artillery. We had none killed and none wounded only those I have spoken of. The firing up the river was across the river at Col. Marshalls reg. at Joyners ford 6 miles above. The Yanks crossed up there but were driven back. I am thankful I came out unhurt also all the rest of our boys. As ever your loving friend

Lewis

Margin Note: I saw a copy of the Southern Illustrated News in Weldon but hadn't time to examine it the first copy I can get I will send it and if you like it I will send it to you. If Bob Kerley is at Richmond yet write to him to send you a copy, for it may be some time before I see another   If he should send you one you can write to me if you would like to take it if so I will subscribe for it   I am on guard and must go to the guard house. I haven't got rid of my cold yet otherwise I am well. I fear you will not get this Saturday.

Margin Note: We will get reinforced to-day by two regiments infantry 42 & 55 NC also a … From Petersburg. I understand the 55th camped in 7 miles of us last night.

Camp Wilson near Franklin Depot Va
Nov 23rd 1862

Dearest Corrie

Yours of the 17th came to hand day before yesterday which was rather unexpected but gladly received. I didn't think I would hear from you until you got one from me after my return. I'm glad you have come to the conclusion to write often, do not forget it. I got my brandy safe to camps although I had a box broken open at Weldon by a train running against with brandy in it but fortunately the jug escaped injury; another box   John Michaux's, a large one   was also broken and the way the cakes and good things flew was a sight, the train ran over and spoiled some of the goodies and a good many we ate   the remainder we packed up and brought through. The boxes were accidentally run over. I packed them up near track and asked the conductor if there was room enough for the trains to pass   he replied there was, in a few minutes there was a freight train come along and one of the box cars caught the corner of John Michaux's box, it being on top, and drew it under the train and tore it all to pieces also Bob Carlton's and H. H. Galloway's but nothing lost in theirs. I would like to be at Zion as you spoke of being there today; if it is as cold there as here t'will be rather cold to be plunged.

Port says he dont care if he is "kicked" as he has gotten use to it and that there are plenty more left. I asked him about the type and he replied that you didn't know she had his, he got a letter from her a few days since in which she said that I had told some one that she was coqueting with Port or rather said it was a member of our company and I judged it was me. I told Port what I learned at home concerning her and another and advised him that I thought it would be well enough for him to drop the correspondence at once as I did not want anyone to impose upon him in such a way. These things do not divulge.

I left your type at home under lock and key, do not be afraid about the letters, father will not see them. I got your letter after I returned to camp, all sound.

I saw Frank Alexander on Friday   a part of their regiment is here the remainder is gone to South Quay 5 miles below.

We haven't had any alarm since Tuesday. Major Ross with a part of two companies went down to Chowan County last Saturday week after some Union men, came back last night   haven't heard what he did   nothing as usual I recon. I will quit writing this evening as I was on picket last night and feel sleepy and bad—will finish tomorrow and then surely you will get it by Saturday.

Monday morning   O how cold it is this morning—frost deep enough to track a rabbit. I wish you would send me a drink of brandy this morning it would give me a good relish for corn bread and stewed beef for that is all we have for breakfast.

I wouldn't be surprised now if we stayed here this winter as we have been reinforced and I think it is the intention of the commander to hold the place at all hazards   at any rate that is what I heard him say on the day of the shelling. To remain where we are we could live in our tents as well as in winter quarters, having chimneys to all of them and with a good fire, make them comfortable.

We have been for the last few days throwing up breastworks and covering it with railroad iron, putting it on double to protect the cannoniers when in action. I understand there is to be two large guns sent down here to place in that fortification.

The bridge across the Nottoway is nearly completed, the train will be running here this week.

Capt. Tate came over after me awhile ago he wants me to accept of wagon master but I don't think I will although the pay is a good deal better, but then I rather stay with the boys even in a shade lower position.

The position I spoke to you of brig. Ordinance sergeant was filled while I was at home   that as I told you was an easy position and would like to have had it. I must close as my fingers are so cold I cant write, I cant fill the sheet there is so much of it.

As ever your devoted lover,
Lewis

"Plunged" was a term for a baptism in a creek.

By "kicked" Port means rejected. Hattie Jewell had corresponded with Port.

Major Egbert A. Ross from Mecklenburg County had been Captain of Company C in the First N.C. Volunteer Infantry (the original Bethel). He was 19 when he enlisted as a captain in 1861. He became a major on May 6, 1862. Major Ross died at Gettysburg on July 1, 1863.

Sergeant George Phifer Erwin wrote this letter. This letter is not in the McGimsey Papers.

A typed copy of this letter is in the George Phifer Erwin Civil War Letters 1861–1865, Burke County Library in Morganton, N.C. and the George Phifer Erwin Papers at the Southern Historical Collection, Wilson Library, U.N.C.-C.H.

Franklin Va. November 24, 1862

Dear Mother,

I haven't received a letter from home in so long, I have almost forgot when. The last was sent by Lewis Warlick. I believe you all at home take such particular pains to lecture me about writing, would be better to reserve some and apply it to yourselves. For the last two months I have written on an average almost two letters a week and I have received from you about, on average, about one every two weeks and yet there are three at home might write. I expect in the next letter to find the injunction I have received for the thousand and first time to write every week or oftener. I usually write oftener.

Everything is quite down here. No news at all. One of the men has no shoes and asked me to get him a pair made like mine. Ask pa to have it done and send them by the first opportunity. To be the same size and after the same pattern as mine.

Enclose find ten dollars to pay for them. When Pa has his shoes made tell him to have a pair made for Ed and send them to me. He wears nines. I sent you a couple of pounds of Soda. I know you are always using it at home and Ed reports you are almost out. It costs $1.50 per pound   cheaper, I presume, than you can buy at home. I hope it will be acceptable.

Please send me a pair of suspenders and put leather in them, but no holes. I have a pair of buckles. If you can dye them some color or other, no difference what. From what I an able to learn we are just as apt to winter in our tents as any other place, more apt if the Yankees don't run us off. We have had some pretty cold weather and I find we can do very well even in cloth tents. The Yankees say that they do not intend building winter quarters but will make an active campaign all this winter. This will compel us to do the same. If we go at it properly, I think this winter will decide the war, at any rate we had better go right ahead and have it done with as soon as possible....

Have you heard how John Duval is coming on. I haven't heard a word since he left here.

All is well. My best to yourself. Your devoted son,

G. P. Erwin

Goldsboro, NC
Dec. 18th 1862

My Dearest Friend

Perhaps before this you have heard that we are in N. C. we left Franklin on Sunday morning and before day light, Monday we were at camp Campbell a few miles above Kinston   there we remained a few hours & then marched to Whitehall bridge on the Neuse river 18 miles from Kinston and 16 from this place   there we took a light shelling on Monday night. The next morning the enemy appeared on the opposite side of the river again and began to fire   we returning the fire as briskly as possible with our small force having only Cos. B & H who were on picket and they held the enemy in check for two hours or more before the remaining part of the regiment was ordered down, we finally repulsed them after seven hours of the severest fighting I ever experienced. The enemy was several thousand strong with nine pieces of artillery and some think that theirs was twelve or fifteen. Our regiment did nearly all of the fighting with the assistance of two pieces of artillery. I never heard it thunder before   if it had not have been for the protection of the timber and banks along the river we would have suffered a great loss but as it was we suffered but little. Our reg. had 40 or 50 killed and wounded   2 in our company killed ... Orderly Bristol and Walt Duckworth killed instantly and had nine wounded 5 slightly, two from Upper Creek were pretty badly wounded. Anderson Lovin & Harvey Shuffler. Pink got a slight touch on the forehead with a ball. The old Bethel stood its ground and the Yanks had to skedaddle with a considerable loss as we could see them across the river we fought them across the river   and by the bridge being burnt we could not get across the river to see what we did but I believe we hurt them badly.

We left there yesterday morning and got here last night. We will be sent to Wilmington or three miles below on the Wilmington and Weldon RR where there was a desperate fight yesterday dont know what was done—could hear them all day. The Yanks destroyed the R Road there and if we go to Wilmington we have to go

by Charlotte. We have suffered greatly since we left Va for sleep &
from hard duty.

I remain your devoted lover
Lewis

Margin note. There was three other regt. At Whitehall but did but little fighting as we had the principal ground to fight on. Two were not
ordered up they lost some men dont know how many.

Margin note. We have had no blankets or tents for three or four days
got our blankets last night—hard bread and raw bacon.

---

*Recently elected governor Zebulon Vance met the troops at the Goldsboro
Depot as they were in route to Camp Campbell.*

Pink was Lewis' brother, A. Pinkney Warlick.

*George Anderson Lovin did not return to duty. He was reported absent,
wounded through 1865.*

*Harvey Shuffler was killed at Williamsport, Maryland on July 7, 1863, dur-
ing the retreat from Gettysburg.*

1st Sergeant Elam B. Bristol was the orderly who died on December 16, 1862.

*On December 17, 1862, Union General John B. Foster destroyed the Neuse
River Railroad Bridge near Goldsboro, N.C.*

Segt. J. L. Warlick

Near Goldsboro N.C.
Monday Dec. 22nd 1862

My dearest Friend

Yours of the 12th Inst. came to hand yesterday, which was gladly received. I wrote to you last Wednesday and gave you a brief sketch of the fight we had the day previous. Therefore I need not give you any of the particulars of that desperate fight you can learn more from the papers than I could write in a week.

We are near the bridge on the Wilmington and Weldon railroad where the fight occurred on Tuesday. The enemy burnt the bridge across the Neuse and destroyed the road for 4 or 5 miles but will not remain in that condition being as the authorities have a large force now at work repairing them. The enemy has fallen back in the direction of Newberne and it is thought they will make a raid on Wilmington and Weldon soon before we can complete the road so as we cant run troops from one point to an other. We have been brigaded with the following regiments 26th   47th   52nd and a battery of artillery under the command of Gen. Pettigrew, he had us out on brigade review yesterday. There is five brigades in this section — dont think they will all stay here long as there is no enemy here to watch.

There are many trains now at town waiting to take us at any time where the enemy may make an advance. We have seen hard times since we left Va, haven't had a tent and but a day or two ago that we got any cooking utensils — got nothing but hard bread and raw bacon, was three nights without blankets and how cold — cant tell you. I will subscribe for the Illustrated News for you soon or soon after. Phifer Erwin has been promoted to Orderly and I to 3rd Sergeant. Our boys are all well and all say they have got enough fighting if they could get an honorable piece without it. I must quit writing as it is so cold I cant write away from the fire and when I go to the fire it smokes me so I cant and so it is all bad. We are all smoked as black almost as a negro. Direct to Goldsboro for the present. I will write a longer letter the next time. As ever your devoted

Lover

Lewis

The Wilmington and Weldon was a railroad line that carried supplies from Wilmington, N.C. to Petersburg, Va.

James Johnston Pettigrew was North Carolina's most popular Confederate general. He is best remembered for what North Carolinians describe as the "Pickett-Pettigrew charge," on July 3, 1863 at Gettysburg.

After the Battle of Goldsboro, the Confederate government created a Department of North Carolina with command going to Major General Daniel Harvey Hill. This arrangement allowed for better defense of the Wilmington and Weldon Railroad, and eastern North Carolina. Governor Vance had promoted this plan since his term began in 1862. Pettigrew's Brigade was placed under Hill's command.

Camp near Weldon No. Ca.
Dec 30th 1862

My Dearest Friend

As I haven't written to you since I left Goldsboro, I concluded I would take this opportunity of dropping you a few lines to inform you that I am still in the land of the living.

We left camp below Goldsboro on the night of the 22nd on board the train but before we got up to town we met with an accident and had to lie over till the next day. There was an empty train ahead of us which was ordered by the Colonel to run up to town and get on the turnout so as we could pass   on her way up she run into a train, another empty one that was backing down to get troops, and broke her engines badly   so there they were on the track and couldn't get away, and we right after the one that had preceded us only a few minutes and crash went our engine into her lifting the rear car on top of the engine carrying away the smoke stack and running back nearly as far as the tinder before we stopped, so there were three trains on the track neither one able to get away. There was two men sitting on the cowcatcher up to within a few feet of the collision and they seeing their danger jumped off and saved themselves.

The accident was entirely through carelessness, the train backing down ought have had a light in front knowing that we were down there, and there would have been no accident. There was a detail made from the regiment, went to work and rolled the car off our engine, got all the rest of the trains out of the way by morning and another engine with ten more cars came down and attached to ours, we having thirteen backed down to camps took on the 52nd Reg. and started for this place where we arrived that night. I forgot to say there was no body hurt in the accident. John Patton came to us the morning we left Goldsboro, is with us yet. Port wrote to Mr. Patton that he was here and if he consented for him to stay he would be received in the company.

We had no Christmas. did you have any. There is some talk of Leventhorpe getting promoted to Brigadier General, he is well qualified for the position but we would regret very much to loose as fine an officer as he from our regiment. he said after the battle of White Hall he had the best regiment in the service and that we never would be exposed to such another fire during the war.

There has been bigger battles than that by a great deal but I dont think there has been any regiment since the war commenced under a heavier fire than ours was, from the fact that we took the whole fire of the enemy ten thousand strong with eighteen pieces of artillery we being the only troops engaged. The others held in reserve except the 31st it was ordered down but never got in to action. Cos. B & F who were sent on picket at the bridge early into the morning fought the enemy two hours and ahalf before the remaining part of the reg was ordered down. The only thing that saved us from all being killed was the heaps of logs on the river bank and the only thing that saved Gen. Robinson's command there was the river, on an open field the enemy would have overpowered us.

At one time during the engagement I was behind a big stump on my knees looking over and a cannon ball went into the root of it, which made the dirt and chips fly like everything and which made me get low. A man from Co. I was severely wounded by my right side in the shoulder. I tell you it made me feel bad to see the poor fellow bleed the way he did. When Walter Duckworth was killed he fell over on Pinks leg and bled a considerable amount on his pants before he knew he was shot, poor fellow was shot in the head and died instantly. I have lost one of my front teeth, it was filled on each side but under one of the fills it had decayed in to the nerve and hurt me so I had to have it extracted.

I'm not very well as I have been suffering with a cold ever since we came to this place and yesterday I had a chill the first I have had since I've been in the service.

Devotedly yours

L

Margin Note: I haven't subscribed for that paper yet, reckon you think I'm a long time doing so. We have been expecting orders to Petersburg and I thought I would wait and see if we did go and if we did I could see some one that I knew going to Richmond and would send the money by him — dont like to send by mail.

Margin Note: there is several cases of small pox in Weldon   there were two cases came down on the train from Petersburg on Christmas day. a young lady and little boy were examined and isolated sent to the hospital. I saw the boy and his face was broken out all over like one that had the measles.

Margin Note: I would like to be at Pleasant Hill today if I was I would stay till after New year and help eat the turkey. Give Puss & Sue my kindest regards. The boys from our section are well.

Margin Note: We haven't got our tents yet — dont know when we will get them   they went to Goldsboro and are there yet. We have little huts made of split logs and dirt something like a potato house that we are living in now. A man dont know what he can stand till he trys it. If we thought there was any probability of us staying here we would put up winter quarters.

Gen. Robinson is Lewis' misspelling of the name of Brigadier General Beverly Robertson. He was a Virginian and a West Point graduate.

John Sidney Patton was Lewis' nephew, a son of his late sister Elizabeth Emeline and Bob Patton. John did not join the company.

The death of Sergeant Elam Bristol was a loss to the entire company, but it was a greater loss for Lambert A. Bristol, his 15-year-old brother. Lambert had joined the company as a 14-year-old private in the spring of 1862 by falsifying his age (his official record says he was two years older). On January 4, 1863 he wrote to his mother:

    ... Mother, you don't know how much I miss Elam, I hope he is in a better world than this. You wrote to me and told me to send Elam's correct ... Mother, it was lost before the fight at White Hall. Mother, I don't want you to think I haven't got any friends in this Company. I have got plenty of friends in this Company. Nothing more, only, I remain

                                    Your truly son,
                                    L. A. Bristol

The complete letter is in the Lambert A. Bristol and Elam B. Bristol Letters, Burke County Library, Morganton, N.C.

Lambert Bristol stayed with Company B until he was discharged in the spring of 1864. He then returned to Burke County and became Captain of Company C, 8th North Carolina Junior Reserves. The Junior Reserves were sixteen- and seventeen-year-old boys whose main responsibility was to function in the Home Guard. During the summer of 1864 these boys were incorporated into the 72nd Regiment N.C. Troops and served in Eastern N.C. At age 16, Captain Bristol was one of the youngest Captains in the Confederacy.

Camp near Weldon N. C.
Jan. 5th 1863

My Dearest Friend,

I received a letter from you a few days since, the first I have got in
some time. I don't see how it is that the letters are so long in getting
through, sometimes I get them eight or ten days old. On Saturday
night, or rather in the evening, we got marching orders whereupon we
struck tents and hauled them to the railroad for transportation, got
them there after dark and we expecting every minute to be called into
line as everything was in readiness for a march   but when bedtime
came on   we took our blankets from our knapsacks and lay down —
morning found us in camps yet   to our great delight as we had, some
of us, just completed our chimneys the day before and did not want to
leave them so soon. A courier came in before day with a dispatch
countermanding the order   so we are here still but rumored that soon
we will go to Rocky Mount on the Wilmington road not far from Tar-
boro as the Yankees are advancing in that direction; but we pay but little to rumors as there are always some kind of a one in camps. If we
had gone Saturday our destination would have been to Goldsboro,
several thousand have gone down the road within the last two days—
anticipating an attack on Goldsboro. I haven't had rheumatism since I
came back nor haven't had but one chill which was a few days before I
wrote last, my cold is much better but not entirely rid of it. I lost none
of my clothing while I was gone to Goldsboro but am out two blankets, one I lost and the other I put the remains of Walter Duck*(worth)*
on and carried them out from the battle field and left it with him
which was buried with his body, so now I have but one but my bed
fellow has several which makes up the deficiency. I haven't the same
bedfellow I had when I saw you – changed him off and now have John
Michaux. Sid Wakefield has taken my old one.

Mr. E.J. Erwin and Mr. Michaux are both on a visit. Have you
seen Capt. C. S. Brown's account of the fight—very correct one, you
can see it in the Standard.

Tuesday

Well I don't know what else I can add, yes I had like to have forgotten, by Mr. Michaux I will send you a quire of paper and a bunch of envelopes, they are wraped up with some that Port is going to send to Harriet, I have written to her to send them to you. If I had any stamps I would send also. Two cases of smallpox were reported in company H this morning—have been sent to the hospital.

All is quiet in camps at present except some excitement about the smallpox I have been vaccinated recently. Those two men who have been sent off were neither vaccinated.

I am sure you will have no excuse soon for not writing often if you get the paper I sent.

As ever your most loving friend,

Lewis

Richard Venable Michaux was the father of John Perkins Michaux.

Edward Jones Erwin was the father of George Phifer Erwin.

Walter Duckworth was called Walter Duck by his friends.

The North Carolina Standard *was a newspaper published in Raleigh by* William Woods Holden.

Camp near Magnolia, Duplin Co. N.C.
Sunday, Jan. 25th 1863

My dearest Friend

I received a letter from you last evening the first I have got from you for some time.

We left our camp last Monday and arrived here the following morning fatigued hungry and sleepy. Ever since then we have been expecting marching orders but luckily have not received any as yet — have made preparations for that pupose by storing up all surplus baggage that we could not carry. There is now in this vicinity a large force composed principally of Gens. Ransoms and French's divisions and at Wilmington and Goldsboro there are also large forces. Should the enemy make an advance either on Wilmington or Goldsboro we are in striking distance being about half way between the two points mentioned. The enemy were a few days since at Jacksonville in Onslow Co. but the impression is that he has retraced his steps towards Newberne   doubtless it was a mere faint to draw our troops in order to make a strike at some other point   my opinion is that Weldon will be the first place attacked as it would be more important to them than any place south of that from the fact, all communication from the south to Richmond would be cut off, therefore our forces in Virginia would suffer much as there would be no way to get supplies from the South. There was a rumor afloat yesterday that we would go back to Weldon or Wilmington in a few days, may be so but I dont believe everything I hear in camp for there is always something going the rounds in camp for men to talk about. Today is the first time I have seen the sun since here we have been — has been cloudy and raining all the time. We are encamped near a Baptist church and yesterday and today was their regular monthly meeting and of course our regiment made a good time out, if for nothing else to see the ladies who came to church; upon the whole I think they were a common looking assemblege, they will not compare with our mountain fair ones as to looks. We had only three cases of smallpox in our regiment when we left Weldon. I dont think it will scatter much as all have been vaccinated which is partially a priventative for taking it, and should one take it who has been vaccinated it will not hurt them much.

Our regiment is in very good health at present. Phillip Anthony was left at Weldon in the hospital with Pneumonia. I heard from him day before yesterday he was improving very fast and spoke of joining us in a few days.

Tomorrow our brigade (Pettigrew's) will be ordered out to witness the execution by shooting of a member of the 26th N. C. for desertion. I understand there has been about fifty desertions in that regiment, perhaps by shooting one now and then it will put a stop to their leaving. Say to cousin J. I was very well pleased with the cheese   I could hardly keep them   when I got to camp every body was wanting them — could have sold them for one dollar per lb. I wish I had some more of them. We are the worst set of smoked men or rather a set of the worst smoked men I ever saw. We get nothing to burn but pine and the black smoke soon covers us. The reason why there is so much pine is that the turpentine makers skin the pines for fifteen feet up the tree which dies in a few years and all that part of the tree that is skined is as rich as it can be and that is what we burn   oak wood or any other kind cant be had.

You say that Miss Rack told your fortune and that it was very good. I want you to write me all she told you; did she tell you that you would marry soon? There is great excitement in camps now about furloughs, arose from the fact that there was an order for each company to furlough one man out of every twenty five for duty. I'll not get any until all those who have not been at home have that privilege.

Monday morning, there is heavy firing in the direction of Wilmington supposed to be at that place. We amuse ourselves now-a-days by playing ball. There was quite a large turn out of ladies at dressparade on last evening, some very hard looking ones. We have the praise of being the best drilled regiment in the service, which make us feel proud that we belong to the old "Bethel"

Write soon and often to your devoted

L

Margin Note: Tuesday morning: The brigade was called out yesterday to witness the execution of private Wyatt of Co. B 26th N. C. T. but to the satisfaction of the assembly he was reprieved by the commanding general. Thos. Parks, Port, myself and two or three others went last night to Mr. Swinson's to hear his daughter Miss Mollie perform on the piano   she is a very nice young lady and gave us some good music. That was my first time of calling on any lady since I've been out. Dont be surprised if I fall in love with her. If I do I will write you Again I will quit and go on drill as the company is now called out for skirmish drill. As ever your devoted friend.

Margin Note: I am not as fortunate as Will Avery — have not made the acquaintance of any lady since … been in the service.

Margin Note: One of Perkins' cavalry was here a few days since — said that the Yanks had taken Puss' beau a prisoner and the last they heard from him he was tied to a wagon and doublequicking to keep up.

Andrew Wyatt, of Wilkes County, was ordered to kneel while blindfolded beside his freshly dug grave. The firing squad was at "ready" when a pardon from General Samuel G. French arrived. Wyatt was killed July 1, 1863 at Gettysburg, "bravely doing his duty."

Elisha Alexander Perkins was Captain of Company F, 41st Regiment. This Cavalry Company included Charley McGimsey, John McGimsey, Will Avery, Sam Bowman, and many others from Burke County.

Sergeant George Phifer Erwin wrote this letter.

Camp near Blount's Mill
12 or 15 miles below Washington
April 20, 1863

My dear Father,

We left Greenville last Monday morning and came down to the opposite side of the river from Washington. Several Regiments and a dozen or two pieces of Artillery under the command of Gen. D. H. Hill. On the other side, several Regiments under the command of Gen. Garnett came and sat down in front of Washington. Literally sat and are still sitting for they haven't done anything yet.

On this side, we are guarding the roads leading out of the town and preventing gunboats and reinforcements from going up. Three gunboats are at Washington, one of them disabled by our batteries the day before yesterday. Those gunboats and six or eight transports with troops are lying off Fort Hill (5 or 6 miles below town) afraid to pass. Fort Hill was built while our troops held Washington before. No use has been made of it since and now we have it manned by our guns again.

The Yankees were bombing it all day yesterday and today but have done no damage yet. It is reported that one gunboat was disabled yesterday at that place. A great part of the time we have been in from two to four miles from the Fort and could hear distinctly. The batteries on this side which are playing on the gunboats at town, are at Rodman's point or Rodman's farm a mile or two below town. I know very little about the distances down here as well as the direction of the different places. Mr. Burbanks can tell you the situation of the places I have mentioned. I know nothing of the movements on the other side of the river. If Washington is taken the troops on the other side will have to do it. We can do nothing here except keep off gunboats and reinforcements. Since Monday night, firing has been going on all the time except at night, and a while ago the gunboats were just opposite us on the river shelling the woods some three or four miles off. They did not come near us.

I can form no ideas as to whether there will be a big battle here. It looks more like a feint than anything else. If Washington was to have been taken there was no need of delay Tuesday morning or Wednesday at farthest would have been the time for attack. Nothing in the world could be gained by delay. More gunboats and Yankees were of course to be expected if we waited. It seems as if Gen. Hill wanted to draw troops away from Newbern. I understand that Gen. Longstreet's division is in front of the latter place, though I can't vouch for it....

... Do as you think best. I got a letter from Capt. McAuley offering me the 2nd Lt. in the company of his. I intend to accept it conditionally, that is in accordance with the answer you sent to Wash. If that is accepted of course I will have to decline Capt. McAulay's offer and will write him a statement of the case. Love to all. I left Ed in Greenville to care for our baggage.

Your devoted son,

George P. Erwin

Washington, North Carolina is on the Pamlico River.

Phifer Erwin's great-great aunt once saved the life of Cornelia's maternal grandfather, Samuel Alexander. During the Revolutionary War, Sarah Robinson Erwin gave shelter and care to Alexander, who was her neighbor, after he had been wounded in a skirmish with the Tories. She then hid him in an outbuilding while he was recuperating. A band of Tories plundered and searched the Erwin house, and when they began to search outside, Sarah placed herself in front of the outbuilding and denied them entrance. She was pushed aside. As one of the Tories struck at Alexander with a sword, Sarah Erwin threw herself between the sword and her neighbor. She received a severe wound, the lingering effects of which contributed to her early death in 1785, at age 35. Sarah Robinson Erwin's husband was Alexander Erwin, a brother to Arthur Erwin, great-grandfather of Phifer Erwin. In memory of her courageous actions, North Carolina honors Sarah Erwin as a Patriot of the Revolution.

This letter is not in the McGimsey Papers. It is in the George Phifer Erwin Papers at the Southern Historical Collection, Wilson Library, the University of North Carolina at Chapel Hill. A copy of these letters is in the Burke County Library, Morganton, N.C. These letters cannot be published or used without permission from the Southern Historical Collection.

Hed Qtrs. Pettigrews Brigade
Camp near Hookerton N. C.
April 26th 1863

My dearest Friend

We came to this place last Sunday from Washington via Greenville
in two days and you may guess that we were somewhat fatigued. Remained here until Tuesday morning when we got marching orders.
Fell in and marched back the road 9 miles towards Greenville—
piched camp and the next morning received marching orders for Kinston to report there that night but to our gratification the orders were
countermanded when we reached here or before and here we have
been ever since. We were all disappointed at leaving Washington in the
hands of the enemy. when we went there we were confident that
Washington would be ours with all its contents but not so   from
some cause or other the siege was abandoned, supposed to be from the
fact that our battery at fort Hill below the town could not successfully
blockade the river the enemies boats would pass of very dark nights
without being discovered bringing in supplies and reinforcements.
Some think that it was not Hills intention to take the place but to
draw forces from Suffolk to weaken that point so as Longstreet could
work out his plans successfully: my notion is that the former was Hills
plan—to take the place. We busted six of our best guns at fort Hill
and Rodmans farm, a few miles above the former.

I received two days since the sad intelligence of my sister, sorry
was I to hear it but God's will be done. Its a debt we all owe and have
some day or other to pay. our family has been distressed greatly for the
last four years for in that time I have lost a mother, brother and two
sisters. I do hope that there will not be another death in the family
while the war continues as that gives sorrow and sadness enough to be
borne; but we know not the day or the hour we have to bid adieus to
this world. There may be more of the same family distant this life before the expiration of this horrible war. Surely (the war) has caused
more trouble than anything that has happened in our beloved country
since the Revolution. Alas! and when will it end?

Yesterday there was a detail of 50 men from the brigade sent to

Randolph and Chatham to hunt up deserters. Reuben Branch was detailed from our company   They are offered fifty dollars and a furlough for every one they catch.

I am getting tired of this country because we have not drawn but one days rations of flour since we came to Greenville, corn bread all the time except on a march. Then sometimes hard bread which is but little better. I want wheat to get ripe soon and lots of it. But then we will get but little of it as there is but little raised in this part of the country and they want us to eat up the corn that is made here and ship the flour to other parts. I would give considerable now for some nice biskets and butter. And wouldnt object to having a little honey sprinkled over it such as they have at "Pleasant Hill".

Phifer Erwin has not left yet, he did not accept the appointment of Lt. In the 7th N. C. — is looking for a better one — Quarter Master of the 60th — hasn't got the appointment yet, but has been written to know if he would accept it. David Moody has been discharged.

I understand a few days since that Reuben Hawks a member of our company died lately at the hospital — dont know the certainty of it.

Our tents have been sent to Wilson together with all heavy baggage, dont suppose we will get our tents any more. I must quit as I have to report at the guard house immediately for guard duty. Direct to this place

Ever affectionately
Lewis

•◦•••

Lewis' sister Mary Ann Warlick died in 1863. Her husband was her first cousin, Peter Portland Warlick.

On March 30, 1863, D. H. Hill began a siege of Washington, North Carolina, a Union stronghold under the command of General Foster. During the next two weeks Pettigrew's Brigade, in conjunction with two other brigades, drove off Union gunboats and repelled an attempt to reinforce the city. On April 15th several boats managed to get through the blockade on the Pamlico River with reinforcements and supplies. Hill's decision to withdraw from the siege was unpopular with the common soldiers in the field. During the summer of

1861 Lewis had written that Washington, D.C. should be a Confederate city. Less than two years later he was withdrawing from Washington, North Carolina and leaving it in the hands of Federal Troops.

In his letter dated October 12, 1862, Lewis had mentioned rumors that Longstreet would attack Suffolk. Now he was speculating that the Washington siege was an attempt to help Longstreet. General James Longstreet's nickname was "Pete." During his days as a student at West Point, Longstreet had grown a full beard that caused him to resemble a campus picture of St.Peter. The nickname stuck.

George Phifer Erwin became Assistant Quartermaster of the 60th Regiment in July 1863, after his return from Gettysburg.

Between April 30 and May 21, 1863, Lewis was detached from the 11th Regiment to search for deserters in Burke County. He rejoined the regiment in Virginia.

Chapter 3

The Army of Northern Virginia

The Army of the Potomac moved south across the Rappahannock River in late April 1863, and the Chancellorsville campaign began. On May 1st and 2nd, Pettigrew's Brigade boarded trains in Kinston, N.C. for Petersburg. At this time, the brigade was transferred out of the Department of North Carolina. On June 1, 1863, the brigade was officially incorporated into the Army of Northern Virginia. Lewis was reattached to the regiment four days before this letter was written.

Hanover Junction, Va
May 25th 1863

My dearest Friend

I have only time to write a few lines by Bill Hennessee as he is going to start soon and I have just returned from off picket, since Sunday morning. I arrived Friday, on the way I got that picture you have been asking me for a long time and an ugly thing it is too, it will be a good thing to put in the door to keep a ring out of the house.

I heard yesterday that Tom Kerley was dead and sorry was I to hear it. Tom was a good fellow. Leventhorpe has arrived from home who is a great favorite in camps. Rations are as usual but clothing getting thin but have more on the road.

I think our next move will be toward Fredericksburg. I will send the type by Bill you must let him see it.

We have more sickness than usual. Camp life has gone pretty hard with me since I arrived especially the eatables not so good as I got in old Burke—wish I had some more butter and salad.

My health is good—have the toothache occasionally will have it extracted the next time it aches. Nothing has been heard from Tom Galloway since he was taken. I heard Lt. Yount of the 54th has resigned and Bob Kerley elected to fill the vacancy. I will quit by referring you to Mr. Hennessee for the particulars in general—will be at Mountain Grove Sunday.

As ever your devoted
Lover
Lewis

P.S. Enclosed you will find a ring.

Bob Kerley, Cornelia's cousin, served with Lewis during the first six months of the war. Bob became a 2nd Lt. On May 20, 1863. Tom Kerley was Bob's brother. He was wounded May 4th during the Battle of Chancellorsville and died on May 16, 1863. He and Bob were in the same Company.

Mountain Grove is a Methodist Church near Table Rock in Burke County, N.C. Lewis Warlick's mother and father, a brother who died before the war, and at least two of his sisters are buried in the church cemetery.

The word "ring" has two meanings. The first is a ghost. Lewis was saying that his picture was so ugly that it would scare a ghost. The second is the traditional ring on a finger.

Hanover Station Va
June 6th 1863

My dearest friend

Knowing you would like to hear from me again I will write you a few lines. The brigade left yesterday but I understand it is coming back this morning. It went in the direction of the White house. The reason I did not go with them I was in charge of a fatigue party and could not get off. Our orders in camps are to have every thing in readiness to move at a moments warning. It is thought we will proceed immediately towards Fredericksburg to join our division (Heaths)   There is a move on the Rapahanock. I heard from passengers on the train last evening that all the troops were on the march up the river except one division; all the sick who are not able to march have been sent and are now coming down. It is thought that Lee is going to cross the river and attack Hooker   at any rate every thing goes to prove that that is the move now on hand. Stuart received thirty two regiments of Cavalry yesterday at Culpepper and the impression is that he will be sent in Hookers rear to cut off his supplies and communication and then Lee to attack in the front but we know not that that is the plan … but this much we are pretty well assured of there will be some hard fighting up there before a great while and I expect the old Bethel will be a participant. — While we were in N. C. I heard so much about the soldiers hard fare in Va but to my agreeable surprise we have been faring better here than we have since Christmas. If some persons, who are always crying out that the army would perish to death, could see large army stores of flour, meat, sugar, bread, molasses etc. they undoubtedly would change their tune.

Has the "Fireside" reached you since I left? — have subscribed for the Examiner for you. Did you get the papers and picture? How do you like the looks of it? Does it favor me more than the other? Thom Parks went to Richmond yesterday to have a uniform made — think he needs it. Jim English & Tom Galloway staid with us four or five days when on their return to their regiments also Baird Collins. They said the Yanks treated them very well.

I tried in Salisbury and Richmond to get your ring repaired but no where could find a set

I must close as the regiment is coming—hear the band ... as ever your devoted friend and lover

L

P.S. Direct to Richmond for the present

•••••

Hooker was General Joseph Hooker, commander of the Army of the Potomac at Chancellorsville. General George Meade replaced him shortly after this letter was written.

Major General Henry Heth was the division commander under Lt. General A. P. Hill. Heth was wounded on July 1, 1863, on the first day of battle at Gettysburg and turned over command to Brigadier General J. Johnston Pettigrew. Heth survived the war.

Jim English and Tom Galloway were in Company B, 54th Regiment, N.C. Troops. In Cornelia's letter of May 6, 1861, she related that Miss Polly McCall had married Jim English to keep him from going to war. Tom Galloway had been in Company G, the "Burke Rifles," with Lewis during the summer of 1861. These men were captured near Fredericksburg on May 4, 1863, at the Battle of Chancellorsville. The Confederate and Union policies of prisoner exchange allowed them to be returned fairly quickly after their capture. Union General U. S. Grant halted most prisoner exchanges after he took command in 1864.

Sgt. George Phifer Erwin wrote this letter.

Near Gettysburg, Pa.
July 3, 1863
8 O'clock at night

Dear Father,

Awful fighting for the last three days, and the battle still unde-cided. Our Regiment has suffered most frightfully. I understand that the flag was sent to Gen. Heth this evening signifying that the Regt. could fight no longer. Not more than 80 men left and they are worn out so as to be unfit for duty.

Day before yesterday our brigade made a charge and bore the brunt of the fight. I send a list of our two companies. This evening an-other charge was made but I can give only a few casualties. Capt. Arm-field acting Col. Of the Regt. wounded. Lts. Parkes & Warlick severely wounded. Hugh Tate wounded. These are all the names I can gather, only half a dozen men left in each Company. The first day Gen. Heth wounded, Col. Leventhorpe, Adj. Lucas wounded, Maj. Ross Killed. Col. Burgwin of the 26th, Col. Marshall of the 52nd, Lt. Col. Graves killed. Michaux, Bristol, Parks, & Pink Warlick wounded day before yesterday will return for duty tomorrow. John Carleton was killed. He was with us looking for his Regt. Jno. Duval is severely wounded in the thigh, ball not extracted, but he is in no danger. All our wounded seem to be doing very well. None are dangerously wounded. Our Regiment went into battle 575 strong. Probably 75 are unhurt. Two Captains & four Lieutenants are all the officers. The 26th went in 900 strong. About 80 left. The 47 and 52 suffered in the same proportion. That is the loss of in our Brigade. No prisoners taken except a few this evening. I an speaking only of our Brigade. Our whole estimated loss is 15,000. The Yankees double. ... Gens. Pender & Anderson wounded. Hugh Tate was wounded, but not dan-gerously (some of the company saw him fall) and has not been heard from. He was either captured or came to the rear, most probably the latter as he was wounded in the arm. I have not been in the fight, been looking after our wounded and a more sorrowful thing I never saw. Poor fellows lying wounded in every conceivable place and little or no attention paid to them. The doctors don't examine a wound unless amputation is necessary or it is extraordinarily dangerous. In fact they come in so fast that this is necessary. Some of our boys wounded the first evening have never been looked at by a doctor yet. Stuart has been in sight of Washington capturing some 200 wagons and 2500 horses & mules. They passed us by today. Our wagon train is parked within two miles of the main battle ground. Ewell is on the left Longstreet on the right both pressing the Yankees back so that their line of battle resembles a V; A. P. Hill is in the center & has not been able to dislodge from the apex of the V.

The battle is apt to be decided tomorrow. Our brigade suffered more than any other. Gen. Heth has reported for duty and our other Generals are not so severely wounded as to incapacitate them from duty. So I hear reported. Everything except what relates to our brigade I learn from general rumor and there may not be a word of truth in it.

I send this by the wagon train that carries our wounded to Winchester and would come myself but wish to see the end of this fight. I have my papers all straight.

I have not heard of any of our friends in other Corps. Love to all at home. I hope to be with you soon.

Your affectionate son

George P. Erwin

This letter is not in the McGimsey Papers. It is in the George Phifer Erwin Papers at the Southern Historical Collection at the University of North Carolina at Chapel Hill. A copy of this letter is in the Burke County Library in Morganton, N.C.

Major General Richard H. Anderson survived the war. Both Anderson and Pender were Division Commanders in A.P. Hill's Corps.

Major General William Dorsey Pender, a West Point graduate from North Carolina, was mortally wounded on July 1. Pender County, North Carolina is named for him.

Hugh Tate was a surgeon with the 54th Regiment.

The following is Phifer Erwin's list of casualties at Gettysburg:

Killed in Co. B
Battle of Gettysburg, July 1st 1863

William Duckworth
A. H. Morrison
John Carlton, a member of the 6th, but with our regiment until we
came up with his regiment

Wounded
John Cannon, slightly
Asa Smith, in leg severely
Andy Morgan, arm off
M. Pearson, severely in thigh
Jim Parks, slightly ...
Tom Moore, severely in shoulder
P. Warlick, slightly in head
Lt. *(Elisha)* Dorsey, leg off
Sgt. *(Lewis)* Warlick, severely in thigh
Sgt. *(William)* McGimsey, severely in knee
Sgt. *(John)* Duval, severely in thigh
Sgt. *(John)* Michaux, very slightly
Anthony P, severely in leg
Anthony G, severely in foot
Keller, J, severely in hip
John Cook, severely in leg
Bristol L. A., slightly
Carswell *(R.R.)*— severely in shoulder
Fincannon, John in head
Landis, Tommy severely in leg
Patton, slightly in head
Singleton, L.
Shuffler, John slightly in shoulder
Williams, J. severely in foot
Walker, *(Elisha)* severely in shoulder
Livingston, *(Jordan)* severely

List of casualties in our Co. today 3rd

Capt. Armfield shot down either killed or captured
Lt. *(Tom)* Parks wounded
Lt. *(Portland)* Warlick wounded

There were other causalities on the 3rd which were unknown to Erwin when this list was compiled.

Phifer Erwin also included a list of casualties in Company D (Brown's Company) of the 11th Regiment.

One casualty on June 3rd not mentioned was Phifer's cousin Clark M. Avery, Colonel of the Thirty-Third North Carolina Regiment and the first Captain of Co. G, First N.C. Volunteers (the original Bethel). As Pettigrew's men went up Cemetery Ridge, C. M. Avery was behind them in Scales Brigade, under the Command of General Isaac Trimble. Avery was wounded but able to return to Virginia. Clark M. Avery's younger brother, Col. Isaac Erwin Avery of the Sixth Regiment N.C. Troops was not so lucky. While the Eleventh was in heavy fighting on July 1st and 3rd, the Sixth was attacking on July 2nd. Isaac Avery rode toward Cemetery Hill on a white horse at dusk on July 2, 1863, as part of Jubal Early's attack. A ball struck him in the neck and he fell from his horse in a stream of blood. As he lay on the field bleeding to death he found a pencil and paper and wrote, "Major, tell my father I died with my Face to the enemy, I. E. Avery." This message is in the state historical museum in Raleigh, N.C. If Phifer Erwin had known the fate of either of these two brothers who were his first cousins, he would have sent the news to his father.

The correct number of casualties at Gettysburg was 28,000 Confederate losses and 23,000 Federal losses over the three days.

Each regiment carried at least two flags, a regimental and a battle flag, and some regiments carried company flags as well. The regimental flag was the flag that the ladies of Fayetteville had given the First North Carolina Volunteers; the battle flag was the traditional blue St.Andrews' × with a red background. When Phifer said the flag had been sent to General Heth signifying the regiment could fight no longer, he was referring to the regimental flag made by the ladies of Fayetteville.

The retreat from Gettysburg included one more day of battle before the campaign was finished. On July 14, at Falling Waters, Md., while acting as rear guard for the Army of Northern Virginia as it crossed the Potomac, Pettigrew's

Brigade and others were attacked by two Federal Cavalry divisions with ar-
tillery. Most of the army had crossed the river before the skirmish began. About
500 men in various rearguard regiments were captured, but the worst loss for
the Eleventh was the mortal wound sustained by General Pettigrew.

After the Gettysburg campaign, Phifer Erwin transferred to the 60th Regiment
in Tennessee.

Captain Frances W. Bird wrote the following fragment of a letter to his sister
Mrs. Robert W. Winston. The fragment is undated, but it was written about
July 15, 1863.

... badly wounded in the bowels, I fear mortally. I hope not. Since the
fight I have in some way made a very warm friend of him. I understand he thinks I acted well on the field. Every flag in his brigade except mine was lost on the battlefield, and I had to bring that off with
my own hand   that may be the reason. My love to all   would like to
receive letters from Mr. Winston.

Your brother,

F. W. Bird

Captain Frances W. Bird of C Company played a heroic roll in the charge up
Cemetery Ridge. After eight color guards had fallen, Captain Bird picked up
the Bethel Regiment battle flag and carried it through the attack and retreat.
The flagstaff was a splintered stub by the time he returned to the line, because
it had been shot from his hands twice. It was the only flag returned from the
charge. Captain Bird was promoted to Lieutenant Colonel. He died on August
26, 1864, after being shot in the head at Reams Station, Virginia. The battle
flag was the one with the blue × on a red background. It was not the Regi-
mental flag made by the ladies of Fayetteville.

The wounded person was General James Johnston Pettigrew. He died in West
Virginia on July 17, 1863. His body was taken to Raleigh, N.C. where it lay in
state in the capitol. The ladies of Raleigh made wreaths from flowers grown in
gardens around the city.

This letter is not part of the McGimsey Papers. It is in the Robert Watson Win-
ston Papers at The Southern Historical Collection, Wilson Library, The Uni-
versity of North Carolina at Chapel Hill. This letter may not be published or
used without permission.

U. S. General Hospital
Davids Island, N.Y.
August 4th 1863

Dear Cousin Corrie

I am thankful that I can say to you that I am improving of my wounds as rapidly as could be expected & think I will be able to throw away my crutches in a month — health good and in good spirits — would like to be paroled   dont know when I will be — will try and be as well satisfied as the case will admit of — pretty good fare and attendance — no. 1 hospital — have good sea breezes — boys doing well — grovel a good deal for tobacco — would like very much to see you
Affectionately your, cousin
Lewis

———

John Lewis Warlick was wounded at Gettysburg and treated for his injuries as a prisoner of war. He addressed this letter to "Cousin" Cornelia because, as a prisoner of war, he was only allowed to write to family members.

This was the first letter to reach Cornelia after the Gettysburg Campaign. Lewis was wounded on July 1, the first day of the battle, and probably captured as the army was in retreat after the 3rd day. Bill McGimsey was also wounded on July 1st but not captured. Two days later, on July 3rd, Captain Mark Armfield, Port Warlick, Tom Parks, Harrison Parks, Sid Wakefield and 12,000 other Confederate soldiers walked up Cemetery Ridge with Pettigrew and Pickett and Trimble.

U. S. General Hospital
Davids Island, N.Y.
August 18th 1863

My dear cousin Corrie

Since my last to you I've improved but slowly owing I think to the extreme heat, but now the weather has taken a change and it is cool which I think will be advantageous to wounds. Twill be a long time before I will be able to walk as I once could.

My health is good. Am able to devour my regular rations — would like to be at Pleasant Hill to eat peaches and watermelons. Know you have plenty would like to hear from home — hope Port is there. Continue to be well treated for which we are very thankful. I hope and trust God will spare me to see my native hills again.

Your affectionate cousin
Lewis

N. C. Hospital
Petersburg, Va
Sept. 1st 1863

My dearest Corrie

How thankful I ought to be and how glad I am that I am again in Dixie. You know not the many times I have wished myself out of the enemy hands while a prisoner and that wish after a long while has been gratified. I arrived here Friday last from Davids Island N. Y. in company with six hundred and ninety paroled wounded prisoners. I would have written to you immediately after my arrival but learning the medical would not sit yesterday I concluded I would postpone writing until I learned whether or not I would get a furlough but the board failed to meet for some cases as others   I will have to wait till Monday before I know whether or not I will succeed in getting one as the board does not meet again til then. I think it probable I will get one when the board meets as I was recommended to go before the board yesterday   wish it had have met.

I am improving but slowly cant walk but very little with my crutches. my face has healed up nicely. I have heard of several of our boys since my arrival who are in the hands of the yanks. Lt. Parks and Michaux are in jail in Baltimore. Tom passing off as a private   all the officers having been sent to Sandusky, Ohio. I cant hear a thing from Harrison Parks   I fear he was killed. Bob Carlton, S. Wakefield, Bob Hennessee, S. Brown and others are at Fort Delaware   hope all are doing well. Capt. Armfield is there also   well. Havent heard a word from Tom Moore other than he was severely wounded   dont know what became of him. I was so glad to hear Port got home   I heard that through Mrs. May and Elizabeth Ann Kincaid who are here with their sick husbands. They are improving. I was kindly treated while in the hands of the enemy but never do I want to fall into their hands again for I have such great hatred for them I dont care about seeing them only as dead, wounded, or prisoners on the battlefield.

I wrote to you twice while at The Island, did you get them? if you did I guess you laughed to see how I addressed you, I will explain that for we were only aloud to send family letters. All were unsealed and read before they passed through the lines, therefore I developed you as a cousin. I know our friends and relations have suffered with grief without description since the fight at Gettysburg for so many thousand poor fellows were killed and wounded, never do I want to witness another such a sight   if I had not got use to it my heart would sicken at the thought. Often since I have been wounded have I thought of you and wanted to be at home where I could hear from you and see you occasionally. I wish that would be so.

As ever

Lewis

Direct through N. C. Hospital Petersburg Va

————•••••————

This letter has illegible writing in the side margins.

Sandusky, Ohio was the closest town to Johnson Island, an island prison in Lake Erie.

Sgt. John P. Michaux was captured at Falling Waters, Maryland on July 14, 1863, and exchanged March 3, 1864. He died May 26, 1865.

Corporal Henry Harrison Parks was listed as missing and "supposed killed" at Gettysburg, July 3, 1863. Harrison was one of Tom Park's younger brothers.

Sergeant Robert J. Hennesse was captured at Gettysburg, July 3, 1863, and later exchanged. He surrendered at Appomattox.

Sidney Wakefield was captured at Gettysburg and died as a prisoner of war at Fort Delaware, Delaware, on September 10, 1863.

Capt. Mark Armfield was captured at Gettysburg on July 3–4, 1863. He was transferred to Johnson Island, Ohio, where he died a prisoner of war on December 3, 1863.

Thomas Parks was captured at Falling Waters, Maryland on July 14, 1863, and confined at Point Lookout Prison in Maryland until exchanged March 3, 1864. Tom Parks was promoted to Captain of Company B to replace Mark Armfield. Parks was still a prisoner of war at the time of his promotion.

Port Warlick was wounded on July 3, 1863. His official records state he was hospitalized in Richmond until he died of "typhoid Pneumonia" December 28,

1863. Lewis indicates he returned to Burke County before his death in Richmond.

Bob Carlton died in prison at Fort Delaware, Delaware, September 16, 1863.

Tom Moore was exchanged on November 17, 1863. He was later killed at New Market, Virginia on July 30, 1864.

General Hospital No 8 Ward A
Raleigh, N.C. Nov. 8th '63

My dearest Corrie

Perhaps you will be surprised to see that I have gotten down here it is even so although against my will. I reported to Dr. Wall as ordered he having no place to keep me transferred me to this place, and I fear from what I have learned since my arrival that I cannot get a furlough at this place, for they say it is a difficult matter to get one. If I should not get one I will be very sadly disappointed for I was much delighted with your promise and did hope that I would be able to comply with your intentions and mine but alas I fear this matter will have to be postponed to some future time. I will make every effort to be sent home till I am able for duty. I had the ball extracted this morning, it was a painful operation but I grinned and endured it. If I should not get home from here the first time I get an opportunity and get there I want us to have the solemn ceremony pronounced. What say you? For I feel like I want to be a married man and if that was the case soon you could be with me, several ladies are here with their husbands attending to their wounds. I know this time would pass more rapidly if I could have the pleasure of your presence, but when will that be? I fear some time will elapse before I see you again

If I cannot get a furlough I will stay here no longer than I am compelled, but will respond to my command. This seems to be a pretty good hospital   everything is kept very nice, good beds and pretty good fare. Give my kindest regards to Puss and Sue

What have you done with Mr. Conley? How bad I want to go home again   cant think of anything else. I wish I had some way of sending you some paper and envelopes.

As ever

Lewis

—•◦•◦•—

Lewis left Raleigh and went home to Burke County for rest and recuperation. Letters written in 1864 indicate he spent a great deal of time eating during Christmas. Lewis' oldest brother, Daniel Logan Warlick, joined Company B,

11th Regiment, and sent home the sad news that brother Portland died in a Richmond Hospital.

On February 15, 1864, Lewis was promoted to 2nd Lieutenant, pending approval. Two days later, February 17th, Lt. J. Lewis Warlick and Laura Cornelia McGimsey were married. Their wedding probably was held at Old Sardis Church. In 1862 Lewis' promotion to sergeant was partly the result of Elam Bristol's death at White Hall Bridge. His promotion to 2nd Lt. was possibly linked to his brother Lt. Portland Warlick's death. Lewis returned to Company B in the middle of March 1864. Cornelia continued to live with her family at Pleasant Hill on the Linville River.

Camp near Orange C. H. Va
March 22nd '64

My dearest Friend

I arrived safe on Sunday and found all in pretty good spirits and health; all well except Logan who is limping with rheumatism.

When I returned I found the old "Bethel" looking quite different to what it did when I left, new officers have taken the places of those who were killed and many strange faces are in the ranks who have been enlisted since I left. Upon the whole its not the regiment it once was but hope it will do better than it looks. The boys are doing tolerably well on the rations they draw, get sugar and coffee about as much as they use. I saw Col. Leventhorpe on his way home as I came out, is looking much better than I ever saw him look, hope he will soon be exchanged and take command of the regiment.

As soon as the boys heard he had arrived they called a meeting of the privates and subscribed seven hundred and fifteen ($715.00) dollars to buy him a saddle and the officers have subscribed several hundred to purchase him a sword.

I haven't been before the board yet but expect to be called before it in a few days. The weather is very cold at present. Our regiment is doing nothing, not called out but once a day and that to have dress parade; but I guess when Col. Martin returns (at home on leave of absence) he will begin to put us through on the drills; Capt. Grier now in command, the Major now on Court Martial.

I stopped in Richmond to get brothers effects but failed they cannot be gotten only by father who will have to certify he is his father with a magistrates signature and also the County seal. Where did Puss and Susan go, and what did they see? T. Moore came through without drinking.

Well Corrie I hated very much to leave but otherwise I could not do, I wish it was so I could remain with you, and I hope and trust that I will be spared to see the expiration of this cruel war so we can again meet to part no more while life exists within us. I verily believe we could live happily together although in low circumstances.

May God defend and protect us from harm, danger through these troublesome times. Give my kindest regards to Puss, Sue, Uncle John and all inquiring friends.

Say to Uncle John Tom says he will pay me for the brandy which he got from him. I remain as ever your loving husband

Lewis

Leventhorpe did return to service as a Brigadier General in 1865. On February 3rd of that year he was placed in command of the North Carolina Home Guard and Reserve units.

Lewis' impression of the new recruits was the result of a conscript law passed by the Confederate government. Men up to 50 were subject to conscription and boys 16 and 17 were required to serve in local defense units. These men were not the eager volunteers of 1861.

Colonel Collette Leventhorpe, 11th Regiment, N.C. Troops. Courtesy of N.C. Division of Archives and History.

Camp near Orange C. H., Va.
March 29th 1864

My dearest Friend,

I am very anxious to hear from you soon and often and I have concluded the oftener I write the more you will answer. I will endeavor to write every week but if you should not hear from me weekly do not be uneasy as it is often the case a march prevents writing regularly. I have taken severe cold since I returned; for three or four nights after my arrival it was very cold and being rather scarce of bedding the consequence was I slept cold therefore I think is the cause of my having such a cold. I haven't gone before the board yet nor do I know when I will, there has been two appointments for its session but other things crowded it out, and now I suppose it will be toward the last of the week before it will be done as Gov. Vance is with us speaking and nothing can be done while he remains here. I think there is no doubt but that I will pass the examining board as I have been recommended by Col. Martin and also have an appointment from Gov. Vance, or rather from the executive Officer signed by the Gov. entitling me a commission if in the judgment of the examining board I am qualified to fill the position; well when I go before it I will first show my appointment, then they will want to know by whom I was recommended (as they will see some one recommended me as the appointment could never have come)   I will say Col. Martin after which I will be asked but few questions; so say men who have been examined.

Today at 10 o'clock ours and Cook's brigade are to be reviewed by Gov. Vance, I suppose, and at 12 the Gov. speaks to them. I'm sorry to say that Holden will get a strong vote in Co. B.

I suppose you have seen an account in the papers of the engagement between ours and the Cooke's brigades, with snow balls it was a great sight. Officers are now drawing the same amount of rations as men in the ranks some of them think it hard but as for myself I can live on as little as anyone without murmuring if the Confederate States can do no better.

I am willing to live a great while on small rations and endure many hardships and privations rather than succumb to Yankee rule, which in my belief will never be our lot. Do not make yourself unnecessary uneasy about me as I am living tolerably well and I will not expose myself to danger uncalled for, it is true my lot as well as others is hard but then I am or try to be cheerful with it.

I will try and keep my spirits up and not fall into deep despondency, the feelings of which is hard to endure. Give my kindest regards to Sue, Puss and uncle John.

As ever your devoted husband
Lewis

William Woods Holden was the editor of The North Carolina Standard. *Holden had supported Zebulon B. Vance in the 1862 election but in 1864 Holden ran against Vance on a platform of making peace with the union and ending the war. When Vance reviewed the troops he did so with General Robert E. Lee. Vance won the 1864 election. President Andrew Johnson appointed Holden Provisional Governor of North Carolina at the end of the Civil War.*

William Joseph Martin, a former professor at the University of North Carolina at Chapel Hill, was a captain of Company G, 28th Regiment N.C. Troops before his promotion to Lt. Colonel of the 11th Regiment. He became a full Colonel when Collett Leventhorpe retired April 27, 1864.

General John Cooke's Brigade had been placed in Heth's Division after the Gettysburg campaign. Pettigrew's Brigade became Kirkland's Brigade when General William W. Kirkland was appointed to command in September, 1863. General Billie MacRae replaced Kirkland after the Battle of Cold Harbor. The men in Cooke's Brigade fought closely with the men in the Kirkland-MacRae Brigade for the last two years of the war.

Camp 11th N. C. near Orange C. H. Va
April 11, 1864

My dearest Friend:

Every evening I'm disappointed in not getting any letters, not one
have I received yet and this being the fifth I have written you since my
return, surely any first did not reach you. I will wait as patiently as
possible for the welcome message. Recently by an underground pas-
sage I have ascertained that Puss has a new correspondent in the 11th,
doubtless the trip to Raleigh was not altogether spent in idle chit chat,
but the conversation turned on a more serious affair, perhaps on love
matters—don't know only guessing at any rate you must tease Puss
about it. I'll lay a wager that you will never see the contents of the
missive she will get about the time or a few days previous of your getting this.

I'm not a prophet nor the son of a prophet but sometimes my pre-
dictions turn out even so.

We are looking for marching orders every day as orders have been
issued for all baggage, supplies baggage, with all visitors to be sent to
the rear; the general impression is that Lee is going to Culpepper as
hurriedly as possible after starting, to pounce down on Grants right
flank while he is reorganizing his army and give him battle before he
will be able to concentrate his troops; thereby breaking and confusing
his plans for an onward movement to Richmond. I think it altogether
probable, if this should be the plan, that we will be able to drive the
enemy in his strong holds around Centerville before he will be able to
give us battle with his whole force. I think it very likely the inclemency of the weather will postpone active operations a few days for
it has rained nearly every day for a week. Morgan starts home tomorrow by him I send the "Raids," to be left at Mr. Duval's—think you
will be mighty pleased with it, especially with the characters, "Lu"
"Mary" & "Evangeline," they were great heroines. I haven't read "No
Name" yet—will send it to you the first opportunity after I shall have
read it.

I would like very much to go home on furlough this Spring but
that is impossible for an order from Genl. Lee has put an end to them.

You told me before I left home there was some things you needed and wanted me to get in Richmond, but when I left I never thought a word about it, write me what you want and I will try and get them and send to you. The boys are generally well but badly clothed, we have had a requisition out for some time for clothing, not yet have we been able to get them and I don't see why it is as there is plenty in N. C. for the troops and now is the time the soldiers ought to have them as an active campaign is right on hand. Tuesday Morning   This morning we have nothing but corn bread for breakfast, we ought have drawn last evening, we draw the same amount of rations as the men free of charge and buying from the commissary is entirely cut off from the officers, all fare alike from private to Genl.

When I draw I will send you some money if an opportunity affords and I would like if you can, by some cotton yarn to make me some shirts   would rather have small checks for I see no chance of getting any from the Government. My kindest regards to all. As ever your devoted husband.

                         Lewis

Camp near Orange C. H. Va.
April 16, 1864

My dearest Corrie:

After along time your first came to hand last evening, which was gladly received and read as in days past. I can assure you it gave me more of a contented mind, the name at the end if no name on paper always looks charming to the one of your choice. Through a note from Capt. Parks at Richmond gave us the pleasing intelligence that Father had to a great extent recovered from his illness; we first heard through a letter to Logan he was very sick, which caused great uneasiness as I very much fear at some time one of those sudden attacks will take him away, for the last few months he has had several as you are aware. I staid with Mat the night after I left home, arrived at Richmond Saturday morning, went to the Hospital where brother died and found on the books his death recorded 28th Dec., I inquired where his remains rested, was told at Oakwood Cemetery 2½ miles distant as I had business to attend I did not go out. I was told that he was neatly buried in a raised lid coffin and that the grave was marked. I asked if his remains could be easily removed which was replied to in the affirmative, said if I could see him I would recognize him as the body by that time had not decayed any. I wrote to father to send some one after them, I dont know what he concluded to do as I haven't had an answer.

I tried to get brother's effects but could not as the proper heir has to make oath before a magistrate that he is such then have the County Court clerk's signature and seal before anything can be obtained; after he fills the blank I sent him, and gives me a power of attorney, with both I can get his effects and money due, otherwise I cannot.

Have you subscribed for the Confederate? If you have not let me know and I will send it to you. Do you get the Presbyterian? I subscribed for it. Do you and Puss want either of the Richmond literary papers? Our regiment is in good health and spirits. There is no possible chance for me to get a furlough this spring as Walker has been trying to get off ever since I came back. Genl. Lee's order is "there will be no more furloughs as the exigencies of the times will not admit of it"

Tom, Bill, Pink, Log and all our boys are in good health. Give my love to all.

Write soon and often to

Your devoted

Lewis

———•••—

Logan or Log refers to Daniel Logan Warlick, Lewis' older brother. Logan was one of the older men with families affected by the conscript law. He preferred to join his brothers rather than be drafted. He was killed at Spotsylvania Court House, Virginia, May 12, 1864.

Spotsylvania C. H. Va.,
May 19th 1864

My dearest Corrie,

As there is an opportunity or soon will be of sending a letter I will write to you again.

I wrote two or three days since but being aware that you will be very anxious to hear from me frequently during these fighting times I will endeavor to write as often as an opportunity affords.

We had a mail to-day, the first in nearly two weeks, none from you. Our command has not been engaged since I last wrote but expecting every night and day to be attacked: the enemies line of battle is in full view, about a thousand yards in our front but I think it very probable he will never attack us in our strong position, if he should he will be repulsed as heretofore. We were under a terrific shelling yesterday for two hours with very little damage. Ewell repulsed the enemy yesterday three times making great slaughter in his (the enemy) ranks. To-day so far everything is quiet the skirmishers dont even fire at each other but seem to be quite friendly, meet each other and exchange papers and have a talk over the times; one came and met Capt Brown of the 44th and after having a chat he, the Yankee, told Brown that Lee had destroyed half their army; there has no doubt been an awful slaughter in their ranks as, men who have fought over many bloody fields in Va. Say they never saw dead Yankees lie so thick on the ground as they do in front of the works where they charged. Their dead lie unburied from the Wilderness, well I wish they could all the time have such victories I consider when an army is driven back leaving their dead and wounded both in the field and hospitals that they have been badly whiped, dont you? That is the kind of a victory they gained at the Wilderness for I was there and know it to be so, we remained on the field till Sunday evening of the 8th and not an enemy could be found in front by our scouts.

We have to mourn the loss of many good officers and soldiers since the fight began. From all quarters we have good news, every where our arms have been victorious — Butler driven back Grant checked, Steele captured with his command and many other places we have been successful for which we ought to give God the praise. In my last I wrote to you of the death of brother Logan   I also wrote to his wife. Bill McGimsey had an attack of cramp yesterday is nearly well to-day. Aus P. has been a little unwell but improving. Pink and I are very well. I am very thankful that we have come out through so many dangers as well as we have, nothing but the hand of an Allwise providence has protected us thus far, for which we ought to be very humble and give him all the praise for his goodness. My wound is not well but does not hurt me. I saw Sam Tate when we were coming down here—haven't seen or heard from him since. We have had a hard time since we left camp, have been marching, lying in line of battle and fighting all the time, are now in the works not allowed to leave any distance as Grant is a sly fellow and has to be watched closely.

Grant is twice as badly whiped now as was Burnside or Hooker but he is so determined he will not acknowledge it, but I think before he gets through with Lee he will have to own up.

I haven't had any clean cloths since I left camps   the wagons are in the rear and we can not leave to go where they are to get our cloths, all the officers are in the same fix, so you may well suppose we are somewhat dirty.

Give my love to uncle John, Puss and Sue. Do you get your papers?

> Your devoted
> Lewis

Aus P. refers to Austin L. Parks, a younger brother to Tom Parks. Aus transferred into Company B from the 41st Regiment and remained with Company B until his capture at Petersburg on April 2, 1865. Aus died in prison at Point Lookout, Maryland, on April 15, 1865.

Lewis Warlick was slightly wounded in the right arm at the Wilderness, Virginia, on May 5, 1864.

Union Brigadier General Benjamin Franklin Butler began a campaign against Richmond and Petersburg on May 11th, but it was so disorganized that General P.G.T. Beauregard had enough time to organize smaller forces to success-

fully meet the challenge. On May 16, Beauregard attacked in a dense fog and forced Butler to retreat in rain toward Bermuda Hundred.

Union General Frederick Steele began a campaign on March 23, from Little Rock, Arkansas, south toward the Red River. The plan was to link up with other forces and break up the Confederacy west of the Mississippi. The Red River Campaign was a disaster for the Union and Steele returned to Little Rock on May 13, 1864.

The forces of the Confederacy defeated General Ambrose E. Burnside at Fredericksburg, Virginia, and General Joseph Hooker at Chancellorsville, Virginia.

Near Hanover Junction Va
May 25th 1864

My dearest Corrie

I have written you often since the fighting has commenced but I fear that you did not get them in time as the railroads have been torn up by the enemy in so many places.

We arrived here day before yesterday leaving Spotslvania on the evening of the 21st, didn't leave until the enemy had disappeared from our front trying to make his way by our right flank.

There has been no causalities in the company since I last wrote. Parks, Galloway and others have come in. Tom brought my pants but left them with the wagon train so I haven't seen them.

We boys are all well. Billie seems to take every thing quite easy. I fear exposure will bring back Rheumatism on him.

We have good earthworks here and I very much fear the enemy will not attack us, now dont think I'm anxious to fight, not so   but this I do know, we have Grant to fight again somewhere and knowing such I'd rather he would attack us while in a strong position as at another time we might not get it. The enemy is in our front, there was considerable artillery firing yesterday and this morning we were looking for an attack but as yet every thing is quiet. If the enemy continues to assault our lines we will weaken his ranks so after awhile we will be able to drive him a cross the river.

Picket's, Hoke's and Breckinridge's divisions have joined us since we left Spotsylvania. You will see by the papers the enemy admits a tremendous slaughter in the former fights. We are all getting lousy.

Give my love to all. I hope I may be spared through these trying times.

As ever

Devotedly

Lewis

Margin Note: I received a letter from you yesterday. Please write often.

Major General George Edward Pickett was a West Point graduate (near the bottom of his class). His name is always associated with the charge up Cemetery Ridge on the third day at Gettysburg.

Robert F. Hoke, of Lincoln County, N.C., had entered the war as a Lieutenant and rose through the ranks to become a Major General.

John C. Breckinridge of Kentucky had been Vice President of the United States under James Buchannan and a presidential candidate in the 1860 election. As a young man he had courted Mary Todd before her marriage to Abraham Lincoln.

Captain Thomas Parks and Sergeant Harrison H. Galloway were returning prisoners of war. Both men had been captured at Falling Waters, Maryland on July 14, 1863, during the Gettysburg retreat.

Billie was William Julius Warlick, Lewis' youngest brother. He was 18 years old when he joined the company in April, 1864.

Chickahominy River
June 12th 1864

My dearest Friend

No letter from you since I last wrote. I fear you have been negligent in writing. The past week we have been having some rest and if permitted to stay here awhile we will do finely. have good water good shade and plenty to eat. We left Cold Harbor a few days since and came down the Chickahominy 3 miles below the York River R. R. for picket duty We are much pleased with the change of base as here there is not a continual buzing of minies from yankee sharpshooters, the continual noise of the rifle is not to be heard, nor the occasional shot from some Parót or Napoleon does not sound so harsh at a distance.

We are encamped in two miles of the 3rd but haven't seen any of them yet, been expecting for some of them to come over. Heard they were coming over today to graze their horses. have seen a part of the 1st 2nd and 5th of the same brigade.

We have heard that Will Avery was wounded and gone home and that Lav Laxton had lost a leg. have also heard that James English was killed at Drewerys Bluff. Jimmie Parks came in yesterday, was glad to hear that father was better. I went out yesterday and caught a mess of fish. Some of the boys found a bee tree the day before yesterday but I being absent didn't get any honey, wish I had been with them. Pink said he got as much as he could eat. We are now drawing twice the amount of sugar and coffee we did in camps our mess keeps a supply on hand all the while. I fear if we stay down in the swamps this summer I will have chills again.

T & Aus Parks, Bill McG., Tom Moore, H. Galloway, Pink, Billie and myself are well. We have 42 arms bearing men in the company more than we had at the Wilderness. Tell Susan if she will come down with her biscuits I will exchange sugar and coffee for them.

Give my love to all. Puss' correspondent in the 11th is all right— haven't been hurt, he is very friendly with me.
                As ever
                        Devotedly
                                Lewis

Parrots and Napoleons were field artillery cannons mounted on carriages. Robert Parker Parrott designed the former and Emperor Louis Napoleon III assisted in the design of the latter.

Miss Polly McCall had married James English in 1861 to keep him from going to war. He was wounded at Drewry's Bluff on May 16, 1864, and died a few days later.

Frasers Farm

June 16th 1864

Dearest Corrie

Yours of the 7th came in a few days since and found me well and enjoying rest that had been a stranger to us for more than a month.

Pink was sent to a hospital a few days since with measles   they had broken out on him before he left, haven't heard from him since.

Billy and the other boys are well. We are in the suburbs of the bloody field of '62—we are in line of battle but no enemy nigh, has fallen back, was skirmishing in our front yesterday saw good many prisoners coming in   dont think we will remain here long.

I think we will keep on to the right till we reach the Southside; the impression in camp is Grant is going to try Richmond from that side, he'll not find it any easier than he did on this. I think we will have some hard fighting yet but not as hard as Grant has done for I dont think he can this summer bring his men up to the strength as well as he has on former fields—think they begin to see the folly of charging works protected by Rebs, and otherwise I dont think we ought to fight them while our Capitol is threatened. already we have saved thousands of lives by sticking to the works and letting the enemy do the charging. May God spare us to meet again is my prayer. Give my love to all and excuse this short uninteresting leaf.

Your ever loving

Lewis

Petersburg
July 8th 1864

My dearest Corrie

Again with a sad heart I have to inform you of the death of another dear brother, my much loved brother Pink died at Richmond
hospital 28th June of measles. Tis hard, to part with those we love.
Within six months to a day we have had to mourn the loss of three
brothers. O cruel war when shall we be relieved of its dreadful consequences   May God spare us of any more bloodshed or suffering of
mind and body. Of five brothers only two remain and how long will
we be spared; no one knows but I pray god we may be blessed with
health and protected from the enemys balls through out the entire
struggle. I was uneasy about Pink as the measles had broken out on
him before he was sent off and I learned by one of our men who returned from the hospital yesterday that he was poorly attended. Poor
brother if I could only have been with him to wait on him in his sickness I would not be so much troubled about it, but here he had to lie
and suffer with no kind sister or loving brother to administer to his
wants among strangers who care but very little more for a mans life
than they would for a dogs. Billy is well. Yesterday was the first I heard
of Pinks death. The mail went out this morning for the first time since
the road was cut—would have written by it but was not aware it was
going out till the carrier came round. My love to all
As ever your devoted
Lewis

————•••••————

*Corporal A. Pinkney Warlick's official record states that he was hospitalized at
Richmond, on June 16, 1864 with a gunshot wound and diarrhea and that he
died June 30, 1864. Lewis' account is probably more correct.*

July *(date torn off)* 1864

My dearest Cornelia,

Yesterday I was the happy recipient of yours of the 20th ult. which was the first from you for nearly a month, and today one of the 5th inst. came in giving a detailed account of the raid. I was sorry to hear the militia acted so badly in defending their homes and property. I wish I could have been there with 200 men, under Col. Martin from our regiment, I dare say they never would have left with their prizes and the glory of whipping the Burke militia, we would have given them such a blow as they never would have forgotten and never would they put their feet again on the soil of Burke. To commit such depredations as they and all other Tory and Yankee raiders been doing.

Billy is sick yet, this morning he had some fever. The doctor came to see him awhile ago. I asked him if he had or was taking the fever. he replied he didn't think he was but that he was bilious which caused the slight fever this morning, he said he thought he would get well in a few days, if he should get worse I will write again in a few days. I think in all probability he will be well in a few days. Think, exposure brought on his sickness; he eats tolerably well … *(page torn)* … a pretty good appetite   he walks about occasionally when he gets tired lying on the hard ground is no worse than he was two or three days ago I dont think he is going to have an attack of typhoid fever.

I think Puss' beau a right clever fellow   he seems to be right friendly with me so from that I calculate he is going to be my brother. I would like to hear the good joke you spoke of. Cant you write it? I will never mention it to him. I haven't seen Susan's lover in a month dont know where he is I heard, but dont know how true, that brigade had gone to Chaffins Bluff.

I was sorry to hear of the death of Mr. Corpening. I also was sorry to hear of the death of Capt. Frank Alexander who it was supposed was engaged to Laura, if she was will it not be hard for Laura and Harriet both to loose their intended comforters. This was together all the distress this cruel war has caused, surely it is a severe chastisement for our sins. May God in his favorful mercy pardon us from further bloodshed and destruction of mind and body. I was so sorry to hear of the death of Jim Conly. I have seen several of Perkins Co ...

Love to all,

Lewis

Margin note: Say to Uncle John Tom Moore paid me ten dollars ... I wrote to Harriet yesterday. We heard good news from our army in Md.

(Another margin note appears on the first page. It is not legible).

In June, 1864, Union Captain George W. Kirk moved 130 men from Morristown, Tennessee to Camp Vance, six miles east of Morganton. Kirk was a Confederate deserter who joined the Union army. On June 29, 1864, Camp Vance surrendered to Captain Kirk's men. The camp was burned and 277 prisoners were captured. The Burke, Caldwell and Catawba Home Guard responded to the invasion and followed Kirk to "The Winding Stairs," 21 miles north of Morganton, where they skirmished with the raiders until the Home Guard withdrew. William Waighistill Avery, a brother to Col.C. Moulton Avery (first Capt. of The Burke Rifles) and Col. Isaac Avery (who died facing the enemy at Gettysburg), was mortally wounded. He died on July 3, 1864. Kirk arrived in Knoxville with 132 prisoners, 32 freed former slaves, and 48 horses and mules. General Sherman congratulated him on his success but told Kirk not to be so reckless in the future.

Phifer Erwin received news of Kirk's raid on Morganton from newspaper accounts while he was with the 60th Regiment in Georgia. He immediately wrote to his sister at home. This letter is in the George Phiffer Erwin Papers at the Southern Historical Collection, Wilson Library, U.N.C.-C.H.

Madison, Ga.
July 1st, 1864

Dear Sister,

Yesterday morning the newspapers brought the unexpected and distressing intelligence that a party of raiding Tories was in possession of your and my home, that the bank had been robbed and that a train of cars had been burned.... And judging from the amount of plundering, robbing and burning usual in such cases my imagination can somewhat anticipate the terrible circumstances in which you were placed. The indignities heaped upon our citizens who have not felt the horrors of war. I am in a terrible state of suspense. These miserable Tories, home Yankees, are more to be feared, when they get possession of a country, than Yankees themselves. The paper stated that an ample force had been sent to rout them. This is the only thing that, in any degree relieves my mind.... I hope to heaven they may be captured and meet the reward their merits so richly deserve.

I shall be miserable till I hear and know you will inform me as soon as you are able ... It makes my heart ache to think of the possibility of your being turned out from your home and witnessing its destruction, though thousands of our true southern men and women have suffered the same fate....

Yesterday was a very sad day for me. Your letters reached me in the evening announcing the deaths of Cozs Moulton and Loretta Erwin. I am afraid that the stroke will prove too severe for Uncle Avery and that he will sink under it. How terrible must the blow be to his family....

My mind is so occupied with thinking of your misfortunes that I can scarcely ... anything else. I wish that matters were not as bad as my imagination has presented them, but let us be of good cheer; the darkest hour is just before dawn. I believe that our country is passing through her darkest trials, shortly to be cheered and brightened by the rising sun of peace; and with unstained...to demand her proper place as a young but noble and glorious member of the family of nations.

I am still improving. Ed has been complaining today of some rheumatic pains, he will be alright by tomorrow....I shall expect a long and interesting letter giving a full description of the Tories. Do write often.

Your devoted brother,

G. P.

———•••••———

Coz Moulton was Clarke Moulton Avery, the first Captain of Company G in the original "Bethel," The First N.C. Volunteers. Lt. Colonel C. Moulton Avery died June 18, 1864, from wounds received in battle at the Wilderness on May 6, 1864. The house he built in Morganton still stands.

The newspaper story about the bank being robbed was probably an exaggeration. No other accounts of the raid mention a bank robbery.

Phifer received a reply from his sister and he immediately responded to her letter. The complete text of this letter is in the George Phifer Erwin Papers.

Madison Ga. July 10, 1864

Dear Sister,

Your welcome but sad letter reached me yesterday evening. The letters from home have contained lately such a continued strain of mournful intelligence that I look forward with dread for their arrival fearing that some additional calamity has befallen you or some of our relations or friends. The announcement of Coz Wait's death struck me a thunder clap. Ma had written that W. W. Avery was wounded, but I was ignorant of it's extent.... The information of his death was very unexpected and very sad. His family has been deprived of a devoted husband, father, and son, our community has lost one of its most talented and respected members and our State its highest ornament. I feel his loss is more to be deplored than anyone who has yet sacrifice his life for his country. It is irreparable....

Sincerely,

G.

Coz Wait was William Waightstill Avery, who died after skirmishing with Kirk's raiders at the "Winding Stairs." Phifer married W. W. Avery's daughter, Corinna Iredell Avery after the war. W. W. Avery had been a state representative from Burke County several times during the 1840s and 1850s. He was a delegate to the Democratic Conventions in Charleston and Baltimore in 1860 and desperately tried to keep the party together. When the Democrats split between northern and southern factions, he supported John C. Breckinridge of Kentucky, the Vice-President under James Buchannan. Northern Democrats supported Stephen Douglas. The Democratic Party split allowed Lincoln to be elected President. After secession, Avery served as a Congressman in the Provisional Confederate Congress.

Camp 11th N. C. Petersburg
July 21st 1864

My dearest Corrie

According to promise I write again, having wrote a few days since and am glad to state that Billy is improving although is weak yet, he is with the command. The doctor asked me if I wanted him sent to the field hospital, that was several days since, I replied not as he could get better attention here than he would there therefore he did not send him off. I think he will be well in a few days if he should not take a relapse; the rations we draw he cannot eat especially the bread (corn)   I have been buying such things as he wanted, pies, bread etc. and for an ordinary pie such as is usually made at home is sold for the small sum of four (4.00) dollars small biscuits fifty (50) cents each and everything in like proportions.

Your long letter of the 28th ult. came in since I last wrote which gave an account of the Tory raid on Muddy creek.

From that letter I see you are very much afraid there will be some of the same character on Linville and I am inclined to think so myself if we should not have protection, but have learned there has been troops sent up there to prevent all such thriving bands molesting peasible citizens and helpless women. I think while they are there you need not apprehend any serious danger as these cowardly tories will not venture into the country where there should be any probability of their meeting an armed force. I am sorry to hear that father has so many severe attacks. I fear some one may take him off. I wish there was some one to see to those mean negros and take charge of the farm which would relieve him of so much care and exposure. I will write to him and Harriet today. I will try and persuade her to go home and stay but I fear she will not as she has told me heretofore if I was at home she would stay there, but in my absence she could not live with those saucy negro's and live agreeable with Susan and for that reason she made her home with Mat. I fear everything is going on very badly at home.

You have given me another lecture in regard to exposing myself unnecessarily in battle, that Laura Avery said she heard I was always in front of the company, I can assure you as I have heretofore that I have not and will not expose myself unless my duty requires then it becomes my duty as a soldier to do my duty although the danger may be great and I know in that you would appreciate my worth, as you would not have me act as the coward for anything now I promise you as I have before that I will not go into danger unless duty requires it.

Yours of the 16th has just been handed to me. I am pleased to find in it that your fears about the raiders have quieted, but sorry to learn of the death of Capt. Tate   Oh what distress in this land of ours. I see you had not heard of the death of brother Pink yet. You asked me what I thought about this being the last year of the war. I still believe as I have for months past this year will end the fighting. somehow or other it is impressed on my mind it will not last longer, and I pray God it may not. What is Sue doing? I'm surprised at her ... over some night and look at the mortar shells as they make a rainbow in the air.

You will see by the official papers enclosed I have been Court Martialed. The detail did burn plank but it was positively against my orders, they did the damage and I am to be the sufferer. Since that time I have been court martialed again on the same charge and specification, the burning occurred a few days previous to the other, haven't heard the sentence. Twill be about as the other perhaps two or three months pay to be withheld.

I will watch the men hereafter and next time they burn any fencing I will see who shall be the sufferers. I'll prefer charges against them immediately in order to save myself. If I had punished the men at the time I could never have been hurt about it but I always hate to punish a soldier, after this my heart will be harder. Say to Puss somebody stole her sweethearts shoes the other night and he is now entirely barefooted — saw him have some letters a few days since and on the back of one I saw "McGimsey" so I concluded it was to Puss. Wanted him to show it but he wouldn't. give my love to Puss and all others who may inquire about me.

Devotedly,
Lewis

Groups of Union sympathizers, deserters from both armies, and outlaws raided civilian populations in western North Carolina, eastern Tennessee and North Georgia. These groups were referred to as "Tories," "traitors" and "bushwhackers."

Both Joseph L. McGimsey and John Warlick owned seven slaves in 1850, not a large number, but less than eighteen percent of the population of Burke County owned any slaves.

Near Petersburg
Aug 8th 1864

My dearest Corrie

Yours last I have not answered which ought have been done last week, but being sick was the cause of my silence so long. I have had Diarrhea for a week with but little improvement   I'm going to the field hospital today where I can be more quiet   I think in a few days I will be able for duty again. If I should not get better pretty soon after I get to the hospital I think there will be some chance for me to be furloughed. Our present position is not very safe, well I don't know that it is anything like dangerous but then a fellow can be frightened so and so … all by one mortar shell.

We are lying in reserve say a mile from the Yanks (our advance being close up) rather gone into camps, but when the mortar and picket firing gets warm we lie low. The mine explosion of Grants was a terrible affair   it was set for us but caught more blue birds than gray. I will write in a few days again — will quit and try and eat some breakfast.

Give my love to all.
Devotedly yours
Lewis

During the summer of 1864 a Pennsylvania regiment composed mainly of coal miners began digging a tunnel under the Confederate lines at Petersburg. In the early morning of July 30th, a large blast in the tunnel opened a crater 60 feet wide, 170 feet long and about 30 feet deep. Two to three hundred Confederates were killed in the blast. Federal troops poured into the crater area and were met by Confederates who took positions on top of the crater and fired down upon them. By early afternoon the Federals withdrew. The North lost 4,000 killed and wounded to an approximate loss of 1,500 for the Confederates.

In the trenches, near Petersburg
Sept. 13th 1864

My dearest Corrie,

Yours of the 7th I have just received and surely there is nothing gives me more pleasure while here that to receive letters from you. After my furlough came back disapproved I intended sending up another, I went to Col. Martin and asked his advice he replied " it was useless if they would not grant the one I sent up in which he said, the appeal was as strong as could be made they would not grant any" so I declined sending any more. You have no idea how bad I want to go home but I see no chance for me unless it should be done through the Secretary of War by my relatives at home and I fear that cannot be done as one of the executors of the will is at home and the settlement of the estate can be made without me   now if I was sole executor the thing might be done. I wrote to Bob to sell my stock because I had no where to keep them. I knew uncle John had as much on hand as he can keep and as I have nothing to feed them I thought it would be best to sell them, some of the hogs are very fine over two years old and would make good pork in the fall but I dont see how or what to do with them. Oh this cruel war it keeps me nearly crazy all the time   if I was at home and could get to stay there I would know what to do but as it is I dont know what is for the best.

I know if the war should end soon or end when it should we would need all of the cattle and hogs. I want you if you see any chance to keep what of them you can and let the remainder be sold. Do Corrie what you think best and it will please me. If they were sold and had the money for them it would be of little use even for the present and two years hence   I dont believe it will be worth carrying not even after independence for there will be so much in circulation it will never be redeemed. I dont know what advice to give you in regard to the mule. I dont know that we could hire any body to keep it. I know that uncle John is over stocked and cant keep it. Do Corrie as I said before act on your own judgment.

Bob writes that Gaither advised him to sell all the property—fathers estate. I dont think the negros ought to be sold as they can be hired out in either case I want you to get one, if sold buy, if hired hire, he or she can make bread for you while I'm in the army, uncle John needs another hand anyway. There is a good many things I want you to buy at the sale, if I should not get there. Dont want to buy any thing that will eat except a negro or two as "rations" are scarce—I want as little of my part of the estate in money as possible. I suppose from what Bob writes the sale will not take place until November   I would like to know the time as soon as possible. I think I had better advise Bob not to sell the negros but hire them out. In my former letter I forgot to state that my second court-martial sentenced me to forfeit one months pay and to be publicly reprimanded, the latter I have not received and I think the time has past off so long it will never come—dont care wether it does or not.

Bill McGimsey has returned to the company although not all together well. I was in hopes he would get home. I dont see how I'm to get any cloths from home as I know of no one that will be coming from there this fall. Capt & Jimmy Parks are complaining some   not very sick, the other boys from our neighborhood are generally well. Billy is improving, begins to look like a man. Give my love to all and write soon and often and I will do the same.

As ever yours devotedly

Lewis

Morning 14th   I forgot to state that John Fincannon & Elijah Philips are both dead, died in Richmond.

•◦••

John Warlick died on August 12, 1864. He was 70 at the time of his death.

Jimmy Parks was James K. Polk Parks, Captain Tom Parks' youngest brother. After the war Jimmy Parks married Cornelia's niece, Louisa Hunter. Jimmy Parks lived until 1934 and is still, as of this date 1999, remembered by older citizens of Burke County.

Gaither was Burgess S. Gaither, a local attorney, Clerk of Superior Court, member of the State House of Representatives and a Confederate Congressman.

Bob was Robert Patton, Lewis' brother-in-law. He married Lewis' sister, Elizabeth Emaline Warlick. Elizabeth Emaline died in 1860. Bob Patton's second wife was Harriet Warlick, a first cousin to his first wife.

Near Petersburg
Oct. 6th 1864

My dearest Corrie

Yours of the 22nd Inst. came to hand day before yesterday, long
time on the way. I think it is the best you can do with the hogs to let
them out to be fattened on the shares for if we should be so fortunate
as to see next year we will need the meat. I think your suggestions
about the cattle a good one that is if any are fit for beef to butcher
them and save their hides, for leather we will need as I failed to get all
that was due me; one of mine was impressed last winter and father had
the script for it that I guess will be lost

I think you would do better to sell your mule for a note payable at
the end of the war in good sound money rather than take bank bills. I
think they are worth but little more than <u>confed</u>. But do as you think
proper.

I think Bartlett is trying to play the underground sail away system
he thinks if the land is sold now while we are absent he can buy the
homeplace cheap, well if it is sold he will pay a grand sum for it certain if he gets it. If I was to petition the Secretary of war for leave of
absence I could be courtmartialed as all leaves of absence have to go
up through the proper channel. Last winter Lt. Dickson went home
on furlough and when he went to Richmond he tried to have his furlough extended by the Secretary of war through Mr. Gaither but failed
to get the extension. when he returned to his command he was courtmartialed   all leaves of absence have to go up through the proper
channel   if not it is a violation of the regulations of war and liable to
be punished for the same. I was sorry to hear of uncle Johns illness
hope he is well ere this.

I think it would be better to divide the property if the heirs can
agree to that, it would be much better to do that than sell and take
money for   if it is sold it will bring up to such a price the heirs cannot buy.

I wrote to you on Sunday that I expected our division would have
an engagement that day and so part of it did   our brigade and Davis'
had a little fight   we had one man in the company wounded not se-

verely, John Walker. Emmanuel Hennesse company D was shot through the head was alive the last I heard from him but he is sure to die as he has lost part of his brain.

I am mostly well again Billy is very well   I have lost all my baggage except the flannel I picked up on the battlefield (my baggage) was in the headquarters wagon and some thief was kind enough to take the whole including my new goods I had just got from Raleigh for a uniform. I am sorry it is gone but I can do without it   Give my love to all

Your devoted
Lewis

Bartlett Sisk was Lewis' brother-in-law.

There was a three-day battle around Jones Farm September 29th, September 30th and October 1st.

Emmanual Hennesse did survive his wound. He was, however, paralyzed.

Near Petersburg
Oct. 10th 1864

My dearest Corrie

I am in receipt of yours of the 30th Sept. was glad to hear from you and to hear that you were well, also that uncle John had almost recovered from his illness.

I was lucky in getting my baggage it was not stolen, but misplaced. I want my coat, 2 pr socks and gloves that is all I believe I want in the way of clothing. I have a supply of shirts, drawers and towels, the principal part Yankee manufactured, captured on the battlefield.

If Bill can bring me a box you can send me some potatoes, onions, cheese, dried beef, butter and pickels if you have any way of putting them up as for bread I got plenty—would care to have some cakes and ginger cake for a rarity. I am very well pleased with the disposed of hogs—was glad you have concluded not to sell the yearlings, but have them wintered. If the property is divided I want you to get an equal share, want you to get a negro that will be able to make some bread, and meat for you. Polly or Clarissa either are good field hands and the former can do pretty good house work. Tom is a good hand to work if he has some one to make him, otherwise he is not. Mr. Parks came to us this morning   he is going to Richmond tomorrow for Jimmie, if he was going direct home I would send my cloth but as he is not I guess I had better keep it till another opportunity affords. If he does not have to much baggage when he leaves I will send Sis a rubber blanket. I almost forgot the suspenders, send them   I could have gotten a pair on the battlefield from the 30th ult. but hated to take them off of a dead man, I saw others at it but it looked like a small business to rob the dead, so I declined taking anything from the person of those who were dead, nearly all were stripped of their pants.

We are in sight of the battlefield, Mr. Parks and I walked over that portion of the field a part of our brigade fought over and we found the Yankees only partially buried, many of them with more than half their bodies exposed, it was a horrible sight no doubt to him as he had never seen anything of the kind before. As for myself I have been used to such scenes and it does not strike me with surprise. Billy is very well looks much better than he has in a year.

    Give my love to Puss and uncle John

Your devoted
Lewis

John Parks was the father of Tom Parks, Austin Parks, Jimmy Parks, Liz Parks, and the late Harrison Parks. He had served Burke County in the State Legislature in 1863.

The battle at Jones farm occurred on September 30, 1864.

3rd Lieutenant Elisha Fletcher Walker, 11th Regiment, N.C. Troops. Courtesy of Eleanor Butler.

Near Petersburg
Oct. 29th 1864

My Dearest Corrie;

Again I am permitted to write you. Ere this reaches you   you will
have heard of the fight at Burges' Mills and knowing your uneasiness
after an engagement I always write as soon as possible to let you know
of my safety, fortunately perhaps for me I was not in the engagement
being sick, the Dr. gave me a pass to remain in the trenches. I did not
do so but followed on after the command as I felt an interest in what
would be done. I remained in the rear till after the engagement. Our
brigade sustained a heavy loss specifically in prisoners. They charged
the enemy to far   captured 4 guns and numbers of prisoners and the
first thing they knew the enemy had formed a line of battle in their
rear. Genl. MacRae seeing their situation ordered the men to "about
face" and fight their way out which was done although with heavy loss
in capturing the guns and a portion of the Yankee prisoners were re-
captured; we only saved a timber and six horses of the captured guns.
Co. B had killed: George Keller, Wounded: J. Gilbert, Lewis Harris
and A. Swink the latter a prisoner   Missing: Lt. Walker, Jim Crawley,
Wm Griffin, K. Mincey, Dock Shufler; D. Short, Jno. Walker and
Joseph Williams. Billy went through the fight unhurt. Also Capt.
Parks and Aus. Casualties in the regiment about a hundred (114), we
still have about five hundred arms bearing men in the brigade after all
our hard fighting this campaign. Though recruits have kept us up to a
great extent.

I haven't been well for some time but now improving. I think in a
few days I will be all right again as I am getting a good appetite. I fear
some of our missing are killed. There is a detail going down today to
bury our dead if there is any of them killed who have been reported
missing we will learn from the detail as the Yankees retreated on the
night after the fight. If we had had more troops to support when the
attack was made I think we could have captured the whole concern as
we got around and attacked them in the rear, had them completely cut
off, but being too weak to accomplish the design, the plan was abandoned.

We have been looking for Bill—I guess he got his furlough extended. I fear there will be some hard fighting yet this fall, but pray God we may be able to beat the enemy in all his endeavors to capture the cities we have been defending so long.

Give my love to Puss, Sue and uncle John and dont forget to write to your

Ever devoted

Lewis

———•◦•◦•———

Johnson Gilbert was reported absent wounded through February, 1865.

Lewis B. Harris returned to duty November 10, 1864. He was captured at Petersburg, Virginia on April 2, 1865, and confined at Point Lookout Prison, Maryland, until June 27, 1865.

Third Lieutenant Elisha Fletcher Walker was captured on October 27, 1864, and confined at Ft. Delaware Prison, Delaware, until June 17, 1865.

Corporal James W. Crawley was captured on October 27, 1864, and confined at Point Lookout Prison, Maryland until June 3, 1865.

William L. Griffin was captured on October 27, 1864, and confined at Point Lookout Prison, Maryland, until exchanged on March 28, 1865.

Kinchen Mincey died in prison at Point Lookout, Maryland, on April 23, 1865.

Archibald Swink, Sidney S. Shuffler, J. R. Walker, and Joe Williams were confined at Point Lookout Prison until released at various dates in May and June of 1865.

William McRae of Wilmington, N.C. was a civil engineer prior to enlisting as a private in the 15th Regiment N.C. Troops. He rose through the ranks to become a Brigadier General on June 22, 1864.

Near Petersburg
Nov 27th 1864

My dearest Corrie

Last week past off without any letters from you, and you may be well assured that I was somewhat disappointed for I always make my calculations to hear from you weekly and I endeavor to write as often and sometimes twice.

We have been very busy the past week building quarters and not done yet—cant get all hands at it as there is a heavy detail every day working on a fort and other fatigue parties, besides a heavy picket line to keep up. We have had some very cold weather, the ground has been frozen hard but now the weather is more mild and cloudy, threatening rain, which will be a blessing to us no doubt as the enemy can not make any move while the ground remains soft; therefore we prefer bad weather at this time. I do hope we will be permitted to remain quiet in our shanties till Spring. I think by Tuesday evening the Capt. and I will get into our shanty, it will be a small room, only 9 by 11 feet, for kitchen, bed-room, parlor and dining room, but then I think we can make it comfortable for the winter.

I have drawn four months pay after forfiting two months pay, by sentence of court martial, which settles with me up to 31st Oct. After this I think it will be somebody else who will have rails to pay for, at least I will endeavor to keep the punishment off me; the money is no great sum but then it would have bought me several dozen supplies and other little necessarys that is not issued by the government. I am about well again and the way I do want some pork and turnips, I think I could do more than justice to a dish of ... or possum either. I wish we could get some nice things from home for Christmas, couldn't some man in Burke volunteer a week before that time to come through with some boxes & I would be well pleased to have some spareribs and sausages for breakfast on that morning. I guess you will have some of our hogs killed by that time. I would much rather eat them at home then, but alas I fear I will not be there. I see no chance of getting there as soon as that. I have not been able to get my measure taken yet nor do I know when I will as no papers are granted to offi-

cers to visit the city. The boys are generally well except H. Galloway he has chronic diarrhea. I will try and get him before the medical board for furlough. Give my love to sister Puss. I remain as ever devotedly
                              Lewis

Near Petersburg
Dec. 3 1864

My dearest Corrie,

Since I last wrote I have received yours of the 17th and 25th ult., the latter yesterday. You say I did not mention whether or not I was pleased with the division and sale. I thought it unnecessary as I judged from the tone of your letter you were and you know what pleases you I would be pleased with. I haven't as yet been able to get my measure, I have concluded not to have the coat made now as it would be a month or two before I would get it then the harder part of the winter would have passed off and in the spring and summer I would rather have a jacket as it would uncomfortable. I traded for a nice gray jacket yesterday—think it will last me a year. If I should get a pass to go to town (more are given now) by Christmas I will get my measure and send it any way then you can make my coat with cousin Rowan's assistance at your leisure, you can have it ready for me if I should be so fortunate as to get home this winter. Capt. Parks advises me not to buy any trimmings as none can be bought that is worth anything, I have a yankee plaid shirt he says will be the very thing to …

I'm not atall surprised at Bartlet's doings. I know him of old, I think he had as well mind his own business and let mine and other people alone. I have directed Bob to turn over to you all monies and property coming to me from the estate and if I should be so unfortunate as to fall in this struggle I want to have what little there is coming to me as I consider you the proper heir and would much rather you would say it was yours than for other persons to claim it. I pray God I may be spared to see the end of this "cruel war" and return home to your side to live a peaceful and happy life, and enjoy the small position we justly deserve. I know I have done as much for the part I get of my poor Father's estate as Bartlet ever did and perhaps more. Money and property I do not crave for now, it is peace, one that will give us peace now and durable—an honorable peace one for which I have been marching, suffering, fighting and bleeding for these three years and a half. What has my craving-after-property brother-in-law done in … I think I could answer back "little"—little sympathy he has for soldiers and their wives, whose bodies and minds have been suffering and troubled, for the protection of his property and liberty unfortunate … everyone knows him who was had any dealings with him.

Mine is yours and yours is mine, do as your good judgement directs with everything we have and I assure you, my dearest friend you will always please me.

I have spoken to Billy about hiring Tom, he says he is perfectly willing for you to have him; you and Mr. Parks will have to settle on the price, he, Billy says he will write to Mr. Parks about it. I think Tom would do very good work under Sip, I think you can get him at a reasonable price, if you cannot, hire him out as cheap as possible, get him any way for I know uncle John needs another hand and I think I would be doing him injustice if I did not make some provision for your maintenance.

I was very sorry to hear of the death of John McGimsey, scarcely a month passes that we do not hear of some of our friends or relatives who have fallen in this destructive war. We have our quarters finished and if Grant and his host will not disturb us this winter I will be more than thankful to him. I have quite a nice little shanty … nothing left from our draw from home but some fruit and molasses.

H. Galloway has a furlough gone up for approval. With medical board's certificate, he will get home by the last of next week….you can send me some pairs of jeans and pants by him if you have the material to make them. The great change in the weather has given me a cold, otherwise I am well …

The men of our brigade are well supplied with blankets and clothing, have drawn recently. I pray god may keep and spare us to meet again when this trouble will have passed away. Give my love to sister Puss and all relatives and friends.

Write often to

> Your ever loving and devoted
> Lewis

P.S. Starney who used to keep Shetlands will be shot today for desertion.

John McGimsey was Cornelia's nephew and Bill McGimsey's brother. Lewis had written of seeing him at Topsail Sound back in August, 1862. John was captured at Hanover Junction, Virginia, May 27, 1864. He was imprisoned at Elmira, New York and died on September 4, 1864. He is buried on the prison grounds but his name is misspelled on the marker.

The men who joined military companies during the Civil War were brothers, cousins, neighbors and friends. They helped each other harvest crops and drive cattle. These men married each other's sisters. To desert either the southern or the northern cause was an unacceptable shame. In 1861 and 1862 these men would have rather faced death in battle than show cowardice in their community. Lewis articulated these feeling in his letter dated June 3, 1862: "it shall not be thrown up to my relations in future years that you had an uncle, brother, or that your father or perhaps grandfather would not...assist his country in this great struggle for independence—was too cowardly, afraid of the Yankees." By December of 1864 many friends, brothers, and cousins were gone. The successes of Sherman's and Grant's armies greatly damaged morale. Desertion became a serious problem. Private Joshua Starney in Company D from Burke County was "shot for desertion" on December 4, 1864.

The following two letters were written by Private Thomas L. Morrison from Point Lookout Prison, Maryland. His kinsman Walter Duckworth in Company B had died at Whitehall Bridge. A. H. Morrison, another kinsman in Company B, died at Gettysburg. Tom was one of the Burke County men in the Sixth Regiment; he had been at Gettysburg when Colonel Isaac Avery died. Five months later, on November 7, 1863, he was captured at Rappahannock Station, Virginia and confined at Point Lookout. John McGimsey had been at Point Lookout before he was transferred to Elmira, N.Y. It is likely John and Tom saw each other while they were both at Point Lookout, as prisoners from the same areas tended to find each other and share information from home. The men from company B who were captured at Burgess Mill probably shared information with Tom when they arrived in the prison camp. These letters are privately owned in Burke County. Copies of some of these letters are in the Burke County Public Library.

Jan 1, 1865
Point Lookout, MD.

Dear Wife,

I seat myself to drop you a few line in ancer to a leter I got from you a short time a go baring date Dec the 15, 1864. To day is too New Years day I spent this plais. A many hundred of prisners that was here last New Years day is now numbered with the dead. The dy from 12 to 24 every day and night. You may think that is a big tail to tell but it is so. There is not 25 or 30 thousan *(2500–3000)* here now. It is a teribel cole plais. The groun is now frose 18 inches deap. There is not much snow here. The wind blowes all the time I seldom ever sea a spark of fire. Sometimes I think I an bound to freas to death. When nits come 18 teen of us piles down to gether in and old cloth tent. We only have 1 blanket a peace and pile it in like hoges. A great many has froze to death this winter. A man that is weakly and got no flesh cant stand the cold weather. I have farid very well for the last 10 months. I got me a plais in the horsepitel. Have plenty to eat and good bead. I am fairing all rite now. Look for me for I will be home before next New Years Day. So good by dear wife. Rite soon.

Your husband.
T. L. Morrison

Jan 30, 1865
Point Lookout, MD

Dear Wife,

I seat my self to rite you a few lines. Have got no ancer from my last leter. I have no way to get stamps and paper. Only as I can save my reshens and sell them. I have seen hard times sence I have left home. I suffered with hunger   suffered with sicknes   with cole with heat with hard marching. Home may be ever so poore but it is the hapest plais on this sid of heaven. I would rather be at home and live on the crums that falls from your tabel than to live a soldiers life. You may look for me home by Fall for this war is bound to end this summer ... There has been no exchang of prisners now for 15 months. I was on the second boat load of prisners that was fetch here. There was only one thousan men here when I got here. There has bin no exchang sence I come here. Nearly all the firs prisners is dead. The avridg death here is a bout 17 every day and nite. And if on this island by body must ly on moldan a way and your faise I never behold greave not after me. Rite soon and often.

Your husband untill death.

T. L. Morrison.

Most prisoner exchanges ceased in the spring of 1864. As has been noted in a previous letter, the men who were taken prisoner at Chancellorsville were exchanged in time to fight again at Gettysburg. Lewis, Tom Parks and many others were exchanged after Gettysburg and returned to fight again in 1864. Grant realized that an exchange helped the south more than the north because the south had a limited number of men and exchange allowed men taken out of the war to return and fight again.

The north began using black troops in 1863, and this addition to their numerical advantage meant an eventual northern victory. Before the exchanges completely ended, southerners refused to exchange black prisoners. Their position was that blacks were runaway slaves and should be returned to their owners. The north was looking for a way to end exchanges and this attitude on the part of southerners made the decision easier. Both northern and southern governments did a poor job of managing prisons. Sickness and cold and hunger were common in both systems; but southern prisons were generally worse than their northern counterparts. As Sherman's army destroyed crops in Georgia and South Carolina and Sheridan's Cavalry burned the Shenandoah Valley in Virginia, there was less food for the civilians and the army, and certainly less for prisoners. Northern men in a confederate prison at Salisbury, N.C. probably wrote the same types of letters to Ohio and Pennsylvania that Morrison was writing to his wife.

Nearly 50,000 men died in Union and Confederate prisons. Thomas L. Morrison returned to his wife and family in Burke County and died of natural causes in 1914.

These two letters are published courtesy of Mr. Ralph Morrison.

Near Petersburg
Jan 11th 1865

My dearest Corrie,

Yours of the 2nd Inst. has just arrived and I hasten to reply.

I am glad you hired Tom, I dont consider that you paid a very extravagant price for his hire although I think it is enough. I dont know how to advise you in regard to the 4 percent Bonds. I dont see why they are selling so cheap, the hundred dollars you could get for it would be of little use, probably buy, 2 bunches of thread — think I would prefer loosing it all together as half at a time — the hundred dollars with twenty five added would buy a turkey in Petersburg Market, so you see what is really worth here in Va.

Say to Harrison I wasnt tight when I wrote — had a good excuse for not being   had no money nor not a drop of the over joyful to be bought; the reason why it was dated 2nd was that I intended sending it by Jack and didnt know what day he would start so I put the 2 leaving the other figure out to insert the day of Jack's departure, and forgot it. I thought of it after Jack started but then it was too late to date it right. I was looking for Harrison in a few days but the mail brought in today an extension of 15 days for him. I am glad on his own account he had it extended but on my account I would rather he had come in this week for I am needing socks very badly. I have only a piece of a pair.

Bob Kerley staid with us last Saturday night, he is looking well, says he thinks he will get home this winter. There has been such a rush of furloughs from the regiment, I concluded I wouldn't send up mine yet while, only two of them have been approved. I suppose you will make some sausage out of our hogs, if you do, and can send me some do so for I have been wanting some ever since Christmas. When I sit down to my meal of strong bacon, or rather spoiled bacon and corn bread I think of the many good meals I ate about this time last year, and wish I had some of them now. The boys from our section are all well, as for myself I'm not as well as I could wish, have the diarrhea again, but improving. I'm sorry Puss didn't catch a beau Christmas. She ought not to let Miss Brown out general her as she has done in capturing Mr. Sid Conley. Give my best to her. May God spare us to meet again is this prayer.

Your devoted
Lewis

———•·•·•———

The Miss Brown who married Sid Conley was Will Brown Avery's First Cousin, Martha Brown.

Lt. Robert Vance Kerley was wounded on April 3, 1865, when Grant broke through the Petersburg defenses. He was hospitalized in Washington, D.C. until released on June 9, 1865. He moved to Vienna, Illinois after the war and taught school before dying in 1869. Kerley had just turned 28 at the time of his death.

On the day after this letter was written, January 12, 1865, the federal fleet returned to Wilmington, N.C. and began an assault against Fort Fisher. Heavy fighting with soldiers, sailors, and marines lasted for three days. By the end of the day on January 15, the Stars and Stripes replaced the Second National Confederate Flag over Fort Fisher. With the fall of Fort Fisher, Wilmington was no longer able to provide The Army of Northern Virginia with supplies from blockade-runners.

Jan 27th 1865
Near Petersburg

My dear Corrie,

Knowing you are always anxious to hear from me I have concluded to pen you a few lines today although it is remarkably cold and
has been for several days, it seems that we are not to have anymore
pleasant weather soon. I have been jamed close up in the chimney corner for 3 or 4 days and calculate to hold my position as long as I can
until detailed to go on picket again or some other duty.

Galloway hasn't made his appearance yet and from what I hear
from the crowded state of the roads, I give him till the first of next
week to arrive — hope how soon he may come as I think in all probability he will bring me something good to eat. I went to Capt. Kerr
Comdg. Regt. last Monday and asked him if he would forward a furlough for me, he replied, no as Genl. MacRae had ordered him not to
forward any more until those who were absent should report. I fear it
will be some time before I will be able to get a furlough as nearly every
officer in the regiment are waiting for the absentees to return so they
can send up furloughs. I fear they will get in ahead of me, but I have
studied out another plan, it is this. I'm going to Genl. MacRae and tell
him I have some unsettled business at home that requires my immediate attention and I wish to have a furlough forwarded. It may be that
he will forward mine instead of some others, if he should believe my
statement. I do hope and trust that I will get home soon for I'm as
anxious to see you. My health has improved but little since I last wrote
— not sick enough for the surgeon to recommend me to the board for
furlough and barely able to do duty.

Sometimes I wish I would just get sick enough to get a furlough
but it may be wicked for me to wish that.

Everything is very quiet — no news afloat except camp rumors of
every kind.

Write often to your devoted
Lewis

Sergeant Harrison H. Galloway was captured on April 2, 1865 near Petersburg. He was released from Point Lookout Prison on June 28, 1865. After the War, he married Cornelia's cousin Laura Alexander. Harrison died in 1900.

The camp rumors dealt with the federal troops near Wilmington and how soon Sherman's army might come into North Carolina. What Grant might be doing was always a good rumor.

This is the last letter from Lewis in the McGimsey Papers.

Lewis received a furlough in February and did not return to Petersburg until March, 1865. By the time he resumed service, Sherman's 60,000 man army had moved into North Carolina from the south and federal troops occupied Wilmington. Communications broke down to a point that regular mail delivery was unavailable. On April 2, 1865, Grant broke through the Petersburg defenses and captured most of the remaining soldiers in Company "B." Lewis, his brother Billy, Tom Parks and Bill McGimsey among others were not captured. One week of fighting and retreating later, General Robert E. Lee surrendered the Army of Northern Virginia at Appomattox Court House.

General Lee wrote the following brief note to General Grant.

April 9, 1865

General: — I received your note of this morning… with reference to the surrender of this army. I now request an interview in accordance with the offer contained in your letter of yesterday for that purpose.

R. E. Lee, General

When Lee rode to meet Grant, Captain Tom Parks, Captain Edward R. Outlaw of Company C, Captain J. M. Young of Company K, and the remaining officers in the regiment took the "Bethel" flag into a thicket. Young and Outlaw tore out one piece of each color (red, white, and blue) and the others burned the flag in a pile of leaves and twigs. Lewis had written to Cornelia of his pride at being chosen as one of the first color guards back in September, 1861. Lewis had followed this flag in eastern North Carolina, Virginia and into Pennsylvania for three and a half years. The regiment had protected this flag on many occasions. The Bethel Regiment Flag would not become a souvenir.

The only men from the original "Burke Rifles" who had left Burke County in April, 1861 to surrender with the Eleventh Regiment were Captain Tom Parks, Sergeant Bill McGimsey and Sergeant R. J. Hennessee. All of the others were either dead, deserted, discharged, captured, transferred, missing, sick or wounded. Billy Warlick died on April 8, 1865 near Appomattox, one day before the surrender. Some time between April 11th and April 20th, Lewis surrendered in a hospital in Farmville, Virginia; a small town between Petersburg and Appomattox. Whether or not Lewis was with Billy at the time of his death is unknown. Whether or not Lewis was sick or wounded is unknown.

On April 18, 1865 Confederate General Joseph E. Johnston signed an armistice with General William T. Sherman and formally surrendered the Army of Tennessee on April 26, 1865 at the Bennett house, near Durham Station, N.C. Theodore McGimsey, Phifer Erwin, and Lambert A. Bristol were paroled in Greensboro and started home.

As the war was ending in Virginia and eastern North Carolina, an army came into Burke County. On April 18, Major General Alvin C. Gillem, a wing commander with General George Stoneman, moved west from Lenoir toward Morganton. The Burke Home Guard, under command of Col. Thomas George Walton, met him at Rocky Ford on the Catawba River. Walton, Major General John P. McCowan, a Confederate officer visiting Morganton, and Col. Samuel McDowell Tate, who was at home recuperating from a wound, put together a force of 70 to 200 old men and young boys to oppose Gillem. These were the same men who had been humiliated by Kirk's raid the previous summer. For artillery this rag tag group of defenders had one Dahlgreen cannon and only one man who knew how to make it work. Stoneman's 6,000 man Cavalry had bullied and looted western North Carolina since late March and Gillem had no respect for the home guard units. When he tried a frontal assault at the river, George West fired the Dahlgreen and the Home Guard shot pistols and rifles. Gillem suffered 20 casualties, including at least eight men killed. The Home Guard scattered when Gillem outflanked them by crossing upstream. The opposition angered the Union Cavalry. At the edge of town, local slaves welcomed their liberators with cheers. One Union soldier shot a cheering former slave; the rest of the black crowd fled. When the Yankees entered town the streets were deserted. Eventually houses were entered and women were "asked" to cook for the soldiers. These soldiers brought the first news of General Lee's surrender but few believed it. Nearly every house in an eight to ten mile radius of Morganton was pillaged. While the cavalry did some damage, Tories, traitors, deserters and unionists who were following the army did the worst plundering. Several incidents of women from the surrounding areas entering homes and stealing silverware, blankets, clocks and housewares were reported. Before the cavalry moved on to Marion, either the army or the camp following looters burned the court records on the courthouse lawn. Although Gillem's Cavalry had black troops, there was no report of black soldiers giving harm to civilians. In one case a former slave showed Yankee troops where family valuables had been hidden but in many more cases loyal black servants helped white civilians conceal valuables. No former slaves were reported as participating in the looting.

In the McGimsey family, the Avery family and dozens of other families, stories which are three and four generations old are still told by grandparents to grandchildren. A Captain Brown went to Mrs. Ann Pearson's home, demanded use of the home and that Mrs. Pearson cook for him and some of his men. Mrs. Pearson replied she had no food and Captain Brown remarked, "we will provide the food." When the cavalry moved on, Captain Brown did post a guard at the Pearson home to prevent others from looting. Mrs. Pearson's daughter was Miss Ann E. Pearson, the secretary of the "Soldiers Aid Society." Mrs. Margaret Hilliard, a granddaughter of Sidney and Martha Conley, has told the story of Tories and raiders coming to her grandparents' farm and ransacking the house. Mrs. Hilliard still lives in Morganton and still has a blanket that the Tories stole, but dropped as they were leaving. Cornelia's great nephew, Mr. Joseph Guy McGimsey (1887–1984), told the story of raiders visiting Pleasant Hill. According to his tale two raiders intent on theft and harm were shot and buried in a cornfield. Mr. and Mrs. Jimmy Furr can show visitors a broken door panel in their pre-Civil War home that is attributed to Yankees plundering the house. The prediction John Wakefield made in Cornelia's letter dated June 17, 1861 had come true, "…he thinks the war will have a bad ending   let it end as it may, and that we will be nearly starved, and the soldiers in particular." When the men who surrendered in Virginia and at Greensboro started coming home, they saw pillage and destruction, but far less than they had seen in battle. North Carolina came under military rule and soldiers were stationed in Morganton until July of 1868. At least three ladies from Burke County married Yankee soldiers. Phifer Erwin's sister, Sarah Matilda married Dr. George Moran of Baltimore, one of the soldiers with the army of occupation.

Lewis returned from Virginia in the spring of 1865 in poor health. He had left four years earlier full of enthusiasm for creating a new nation. As time passed his tone changed to "end the war with honor," and finally it became "if I can just return to see my native hills again." When he arrived in Burke County the armies he had fought were an occupation force in his home, but the hills and mountains still had the beauty he remembered. His wife was waiting to begin a new life after the war.

Lewis died July 9, 1865, less than three months after his surrender in Virginia. Cornelia buried him at Mt. Grove Methodist Church next to a brother who died before the war and near his mother and father. As of this date, his tombstone is broken and his grave is unmarked. He was 31 years old at the time of his passing, and the last of five brothers who served in the same company from Burke County.

Epilogue

Cornelia received (and rejected) proposals of marriage from at least five suitors, beginning less than a year after Lewis' death. Several letters from these gentlemen survive. The following two letters are from William Brown Avery, who eventually won her hand.

Canoe Hill March 22nd/68

Dear Cornelia

Please excuse and forgive my forgetfulness in bringing those articles home with me, which you gave me in the store the other evening to put in my pocket, my only plea of excuse for so doing is that when I am in your pleasant society, I forget myself entirely and am carried away beyond the power of self control. I was in Morganton yesterday, took dinner with our cousin Puss and Bob. brought Sol home in the evening heard Dr. Miller preach a capital sermon. Puss rowed me up Salt River in high style, but I do not care for her teasing. I will tell you all about it when I see you, which I hope will be soon. I cannot tell you positively whether I can be up on Linville to see you this week or not. Will do so if I possibly can, for I certainly wish to see you very much, your superior mind and good sense, will cause you to keep this note strictly private I remain as ever your true and <u>affectionate friend, W. B. Avery.</u>

This letter is not in the McGimsey Papers. It is privately owned in North Carolina.

Canoe Hill, Burke County, N.C., as it appeared in 1998.

Canoe Hill April 13th /68

Dear Cornelia

O what a dark, gloomy, rainy dull day. If I had not been employed doing some little something for mother, I would certainly have taken the blues, I did have the blues yesterday evening, The rain prevented any of us from going to McDowels Chapel and I passed a ... unpleasant evening, I took dinners down at Aunt Sophias today with Puss & Bob & Sol., Puss told me that my first duty was to my mother, I told her that I had been thinking of it. I had come to the conclusion it was a very hard duty. If my countenance betrays the feelings of my heart, I certainly must have presented an woeful appearance to you when I left you yesterday evening, for I was sorry and grieved that circumstances did not present me to accompany you home. And now it is Monday evening and I do not know whether you reached home at all yesterday. Only your Cousin Bob told me, he would see it was alright so far as you were concerned, I mean that he would attend upon you when I told him I could not go with you to Linville. Dear Cornelia I did not know that it would work so strong upon my feelings until after I left you yesterday to be compelled to go off and leave one whom I Love so tenderly without being able to protect and shield her from the inclemency of the weather was something I had not experienced before. You know that our private affair at this time to me at least is not in a very enviable position hope & fear prevail alternately, but I will hope that you are thinking favorably of my case. I have indeed spent many pleasant hours with you of late and can truly say from the bottom of my heart the more I see and know of you the more tenderly I Love You.

Dear Cornelia it is now past 8 oclock   Laura, Mother & Puss have all retired and I am sitting here in my room engaged in the pleasing task of writing a letter to the one I love best on this Earth, how I have wished to say many many times that I have been with you, but I will try and see you before many days. You recollect what you told me walking down to the church yesterday, about Mr. Bowman going home with me from the speaking Friday, well Theodore McGimsey told me when I came out of the church that he heard I was ... If Sol

Caster comes up here tomorrow, I will send you this letter, but if he does not come I will have to go and take it myself to you which would be much more pleasant to me now. My dear Cornelia Sol will do to trust, he can keep a secret, I know this to be so, and I would love so much to hear from you when Sol returns, you could do that privately without compromising your dignity or self respect in the least. I would love so much to know that your feeling and your sentiments towards me had not changed since I last parted with you at Pleasant Hill. I would also like to know that you do not censure me for anything done on yesterday at church. Now please be a <u>dear good sweet pretty girl</u>   and write me a little note, by Sol, it will do me so much good and Sol will keep it silent as the grave. But if you think it would be amiss to do so, of course I must submit patiently until I see you. It is now bedtime and I have wrote more than I expected when I commenced. I will close good night, pleasant dreams attend you, I remain your affectionate lover.

W. B. Avery

P. S. I forgot to tell you that I loaned my hat to Pastor Resnall Sunday on my way home from church and my head got a little wet when I took my horse out and it gave me sore throat and cold. Goody bye,

W. B. A.

This Puss was Cornelia's cousin Susan Elizabeth Alexander, daughter of Robert and Sophie Alexander. Cornelia had mentioned her in letters she wrote during the summer of 1861.

Cornelia first mentioned Will Avery in her letter dated June 17, 1861. Lewis mentioned him on several occasions.

This letter is not in the McGimsey Papers. It is printed here courtesy of Mrs. Jimmy Furr.

Will and Laura Cornelia Avery. Courtesy of Mrs. Jimmy Furr.

Laura Cornelia McGimsey Warlick married William Brown Avery on November 16, 1868 and made her home at Canoe Hill, in Burke County, N.C. Their six children were Joseph Waightstill Avery, William Harrison Avery, Elizabeth Brown Avery, Laura Ophelia Avery, Robert James Avery, and Alexander Leighton Avery. William Harrison Avery married Mary Addie Warlick, a daughter of Pinkney A. Warlick on February 26, 1908. Pinkney Warlick was a double first cousin to J. Lewis Warlick and Lewis had mentioned this cousin in a letter dated July 21, 1862. Some descendants of this Avery-Warlick union still live at Swan Ponds, a property which has been owned by either Averys or Warlicks since the 1700s. Canoe Hill is still owned by other members of the Avery family. Elizabeth Brown Avery was responsible for these letters being in the Southern Historical Collection, Wilson Library, U.N.C.-C.H.

Celeste Ophelia McGimsey (Puss) married Daniel G. Carter of Burnsville, N.C. in 1880. Her husband died in 1886 and left Puss a widow with a son and two daughters. One daughter was named Cornelia and the other was Ophelia. Her son Daniel Jennings Carter became a newspaper publisher in North Wilkesboro, N.C.

John Wakefield (Uncle John) died in 1875 and was buried in the McGimsey family cemetery at Pleasant Hill. After his death, Alpheus McGimsey and his family owned Pleasant Hill until the Southern Power Company (Duke Power) bought the property for Lake James in 1916. The old house burned to the ground in late summer, 1999. The rooms where Corrie wrote and read her letters are ashes. Only the hearths and chimneys still stand near the Linville River.

Sergeant Bill McGimsey returned home and married twice. His first wife was Eveline Conley and his second wife was her cousin, Ada Conley. He had six children by both marriages. Bill was one of four brothers who fought in the Civil War. One brother did not return. Bill McGimsey died in 1924.

Captain Tom Parks came home from the war and married Will Avery's sister Harriet on October 22, 1867. For a short time Tom Parks and Cornelia were brother and sister-in-law. Harriet Avery Parks died in childbirth on February 3, 1869. Tom's second wife was Louisa Neal. Tom was one of six brothers who served during the war. Two of his brothers did not return. Tom Parks died in 1912.

George Phifer Erwin practiced law, then became President of the Piedmont Bank in Morganton. He died in 1911. His daughter Adelaide (Mrs. William Elliott White) presented his papers to the Southern Historical Collection.

William Woods Holden, the editor of *The North Carolina Standard* who was appointed provisional Governor after the war, was finally elected in his own right in 1868. In 1870 Holden declared martial law in Alamance and Caswell Counties because of Klu Klux Klan murder and violence. He sent Col. George Kirk (the same George Kirk who had led a raid into Burke County in the summer of 1864) with the State Militia to put down the Klan activity. A Democratically controlled state legislature responded with impeachment. Holden was impeached in 1871 on six of eight counts of high crimes and misdemeanors. He is the only Governor of North Carolina to be impeached. Holden's successor was Lt. Governor Tod R. Caldwell from Burke County. His wife Minerva, the former Treasurer of "The Soldiers Aid Society of Burke County" became First Lady of North Carolina.

Riley Rufus McGimpsey, a slave who had grown up at Pleasant Hill during the time Cornelia was writing to Lewis, married Christian V. Moore in 1871. Their oldest daughter in a family of 10 children was named Cornelia. Riley and Christina acquired land near Pleasant Hill and were neighbors with Alpheus McGimsey's family. Riley was a good farmer, a good businessman, a leader in his church, and a responsible citizen who worked to educate the children in his community. Some of the letters Christina wrote to Riley while he was working away from the home survive. These letters describe events at home in much the same way that Cornelia's letters described events to Lewis. Riley McGimpsey expressed a sense of good will toward his fellow man and did his part in making the community a better place. He died in 1934, shortly after turning 90.

On August 24th, 1911, the cornerstone for the Burke County Confederate Monument was laid on the courthouse lawn in Morganton. More than 200 Veterans and "acres" of citizens attended the festivities to honor the old men who fought and old women who supported them. Some of those old veterans were mentioned in these letters. The veteran who organized the exercise was Capt. Lambert A. Bristol, the 15-year-old private who had seen his brother die at White Hall Bridge and then become one of the youngest company captains in the Confederacy. Once more the old men dressed in gray and taupe and marched around the Courthouse Square to the music from a band. Once more they listened to men from Raleigh make orations. Then they enjoyed a picnic feast on the grounds. If Cornelia was present that day she was honored as a widow of two confederate veterans and as a patriot on the home front.

On May 10, 1919 Captain Edward Outlaw, Company C Eleventh Regiment, presented the three pieces of the Bethel Regiment Flag, which had

Laura Corneila McGimsey Warlick Avery in later years. Courtesy of Mrs. Jimmy Furr.

been removed at Appomattox to the North Carolina Museum of History as a loan. Miss Sue Capehart of Bertie County sewed the three colors together with a fringe. The size of the flag remnant was 4½ inches by 3½ inches. A letter written in March of 1978 stated the remnant was missing or stolen.

When Cornelia died in 1920, she was buried in the Avery family cemetery next to her husband. Very near her is Harrison Avery's marker. Cornelia had written about his funeral in her letter dated August 21, 1861. Another nearby marker is that of Harriet Parks, wife of Captain Tom Parks. Tom's unnamed infant son also has a marker.

Sources

Barrett, John G. *North Carolina as a Civil War Battleground 1861–1865*, Raleigh: Division of Archives and History, 1987.

Blue & Gray, Vol. XVI, issue 2. Columbus, Ohio. 1998.

The Burke Journal, Vol. XVI No. 4. Morganton, N.C. Reprinted from The News Herald, Morganton, N.C. Thursday, August 31, 1911.

Catton, Bruce. *Terrible Swift Sword*, Garden City, N.Y: Doubleday & Company, 1963.

Chapman, Craig S. *More Terrible than Victory, North Carolina's Bloody Bethel Regiment*, Washington: Brassey's, 1998.

Clark, Walter. *Histories of the Several Regiments and Battalions from North Carolina in the Great War, 1861–1865*. 5 Vol., Raleigh, N.C., E. M. Uzzel, 1901. Reprinted by Broadfoot Publishing, Wilmington, 1996.

Compiled Service Records, 11th Regiment, N.C. Troops. Microfilm, National Archives, Washington, D.C. Copies in the state Archives and History.

Dunn, Rachel Warlick. *Daniel Warlick of Lincoln County and his Descendants*. Charlotte: Delmar Printing, 1983.

Freeman, Douglas Southall. *Lee's Lieutenants*, 3 Vols. New York: Charles Scribner's Sons, 1944.

de Gast, Robert. *Lighthouses of the Chesapeake*. Baltimore: Johns Hopkins Press, 1973.

Grant, Ulysses S. *The Personal Memoirs and Selected Letters of Ulysses S. Grant*, New York: Literary Classics of the United States, 1990. Reprinted from *The Papers of Ulysses S. Grant*, Edited by John Y Simon, Vol. 1–14 Southern Illinois University Press, 1967–1985.

Heritage of Burke County 1981, Comp. Morganton: Burke County Historical Society. 1981. Contributors: Isaac Thomas Avery, Jr.; Jean C. Ervin, Ph.D.; Eunice W. Ervin; Sam J. Ervin, Jr.; Millie Fox Harbison; Pinkney L. Lackey; Margaret E. McGimsey; W. Erwin McGimsey; Nettie McGimpsey McIntosh; R. P. Moore; Mildred Beck Taylor; Elizabeth Avery Verble; Sam Wakefield; Kenneth Warlick; William E. White. Jr., M.D.

Heritage of Craven County, Vol. 1, 1984, Comp. New Bern: Eastern North Carolina Genealogical Society.

Huggins, Edith Warren. *The McGimsey Family*, 1962. Manuscript copy in the genealogy room, N.C. Archives and History.

Linville Methodist Church. *The First 100 Years, Centennial Commemoration, 1874–1974*. Morganton, N.C., 1974.

Long, Everette B. *The Civil War Day by Day: An Almanac 1861–1865.* New York: DaCapo Press, 1971.

Manarin, Louis H., and Weymouth T. Jordan, Comp. *North Carolina Troops 1861–1865: A Roster.* 14 Vols. Raleigh, 1966–1998.

The News Herald, Morganton, N.C. Thursday, November 28, 1935, Woman's Club Edition, Page 9.

The North Carolina Standard, Raleigh, N.C. December 21, 1862.

van Noppen, Ina W. "The Significance of Stoneman's Last Raid," *North Carolina Historical Review*, January–October 1961.

Phifer, Edward William, Jr. *Burke: The History of a North Carolina County*, privately published, Morganton, N.C. 1977.

———. *Saga of A Burke County Family: The Averys*. Raleigh, N.C. The North Carolina Department of Cultural Resources, Division of Archives and History. Reprinted from *The North Carolina Historical Review*, Winter, Spring and Summer issues. 1962.

Powell, William S. *North Carolina through Four Centuries*, Chapel Hill: University of North Carolina Press. 1989.

Sandburg, Carl. *Abraham Lincoln: The Prairie Years and the War Years*, New York. Galahad Books. 1993.

Shirley, Franklin Ray. *Zebulon Vance, Tarheel Spokesman*, Charlotte, N.C.: Heritage Printers, Inc. 1962.

Trotter, William R. *Bushwhackers! The Civil War in North Carolina,* Vol. 11: *The Mountains.* Greensboro. Signal Research, Inc. 1988.

Watson, Alan D. *Wilmington: Port of North Carolina.* Columbia: University of South Carolina Press, 1992.

White, Emmett R. *Revolutionary War Soldiers of Western North Carolina: Burke County*, Vol. 1. Easley, S.C. Southern Historical Press, 1984.

Wilson, Clyde N. *Carolina Cavalier: The Life and Mind of James Johnston Pettigrew*, Athens, Ga.: University of Georgia Press, 1990.

Index